OPTIONS TRADING

PSYCHOLOGY

The Art of Mastering Your Trading Mindset for Financial Freedom

- KARTHIK MUTHUMOHAN
- VIGNESH MUTHUMOHAN

Disclaimer:

The contents of this work are intended solely for educational and informational purposes. None of the information presented here should be considered as investment advice for trading or investing in any securities or as medical advice for self-diagnosis. Prior to making any financial decisions, it is crucial to consult with your financial advisor, and before taking any medications, seek guidance from a healthcare professional. The author and the publisher disclaim any responsibility for damages resulting from the advice provided in this publication.

This work is grounded in current events, corporate filings, and the collective experiences of traders. While extensive efforts have been made to ensure accuracy, errors may exist. Readers are strongly advised not to base investment or medical decisions solely on the information contained in this publication. Ultimately, the responsibility for your financial and health-related choices lies with you, the reader.

Table of Contents

INTRODUCTION

Welcome to the intriguing and complex world of options trading, where fortunes can be made or lost in the blink of an eye. Behind the numbers, charts, and strategies lies a critical element that often separates the successful from the struggling trader: psychology. The human mind, with its intricate web of emotions, biases, and instincts, plays an undeniable role in shaping the outcomes of options trading. This book, "Options Trading Psychology," is your guide to understanding and mastering this elusive but essential aspect of the trading game.

Options trading is often regarded as one of the most versatile and powerful tools in the financial markets. It offers a unique array of strategies that can be tailored to various market conditions and risk appetites, making it a playground for those seeking to capitalize on price movements, hedge against risk, or generate income. However, the potential for success in options trading is not limited to your ability to comprehend complex strategies or analyze market data— it hinges significantly on your capacity to manage your own mind.

Why, you might wonder, is psychology so pivotal in the realm of options trading? The answer lies in the inherent nature of financial markets themselves. Markets are not mere machines, but rather dynamic ecosystems fueled by the emotions, decisions, and actions of countless participants worldwide. As an options trader, you are a part of this vast network, and your psychological state can influence not only your own trades but also the broader market sentiment.

Picture this: You have meticulously analyzed the market, conducted extensive research, and devised a flawless options strategy. Yet, when it comes time to execute your plan, fear seizes you. You hesitate, second-guess yourself, and ultimately make decisions that deviate from your well-thought-out strategy. This scenario is all too familiar to many traders. It underscores the undeniable truth that options trading is not solely about market analysis; it's equally about mastering your own mind.

In "Options Trading Psychology," we embark on a transformative journey into the intricate web of thoughts, emotions, and behaviors that shape your trading decisions. We will explore the depths of fear, greed, discipline, and self-control. We will uncover the cognitive biases that lead traders astray and learn how to navigate through the stormy seas of uncertainty with poise and resilience.

This book is not just a theoretical exploration of trading psychology; it's a practical guide that equips you with actionable strategies and techniques to enhance your trading mindset. Whether you are a novice trader looking to build a solid foundation or an experienced professional seeking to sharpen your psychological edge, you will find valuable insights and tools here.

Throughout the following chapters, we will delve into the realms of emotional intelligence, risk management, discipline, patience, and self-reflection. We will share real-life stories of triumphs and setbacks from seasoned traders and reveal their psychological secrets to success. You will discover how mindfulness, stress management, and self-awareness can be powerful allies on your trading journey. We will also explore the intricate relationship between your physical well-being and trading performance.

"Options Trading Psychology" is more than just a book; it's your trusted companion on the path to becoming a more composed, confident, and successful options trader. As we navigate the complex terrain of trading psychology together, remember that the journey itself is as important as the destination. Your quest for self-mastery in trading will not only impact your financial well-being but also the way you approach challenges and uncertainties in life.

So, fasten your seatbelt, dear reader, and prepare to embark on a voyage that will transform not only your trading career but also your relationship with the intricate landscape of your own mind. Let's embark on this enlightening journey into the heart and soul of options trading psychology, where the potential for growth and self-discovery is as boundless as the markets themselves.

1. The Trader's Mind: Unveiling the Psychology of Options Trading

In the intriguing world of options trading, the human mind takes center stage, influencing every decision made in the pursuit of profit and success. Within this chapter, we embark on a captivating journey through the diverse mindsets that traders bring to the options trading arena. From the audacious "Get-Rich-Quick" mindset to the cautious "Derivatives Skeptic" viewpoint, each mindset paints a unique portrait of how traders approach this complex financial landscape. Together, these mindsets form a rich tapestry that reveals the intricate psychology underpinning options trading, guiding us toward a deeper understanding of the trader's psyche.

The Get-Rich-Quick Mindset
  - This mindset is characterized by the desire for rapid financial gains without a clear plan. Traders with this mindset often enter options trading with unrealistic expectations of doubling or tripling their capital overnight.

  - Example: John, a novice trader, hears about options trading from a friend who claims to have made significant profits in a short time. Excited by the idea of quick wealth, John invests a substantial portion of his savings in speculative options contracts without understanding the risks. He experiences significant losses and regrets his impulsive decisions.

The Cautious Investor Mindset
  - Traders with a cautious mindset prioritize capital preservation and may initially opt for conservative strategies like covered calls or protective puts. They focus on minimizing risk and avoiding large losses.

- Example: Sarah, a risk-averse investor, decides to dip her toes into options trading. She starts by selling covered calls on a stock she already owns. While her gains are modest compared to riskier strategies, she appreciates the steady income and peace of mind that comes with limiting her exposure to losses.

The Speculative Gambler Mindset

- This mindset equates options trading with high-stakes gambling. Traders may view options as lottery tickets, hoping for huge payoffs without a clear strategy.

- Example: Mike, inspired by stories of overnight millionaires in the options market, starts buying out-of-the-money call options on speculative stocks. He places bets with money he can't afford to lose, hoping for a big win. Unfortunately, most of his options expire worthless, leading to substantial losses.

The Learning and Growth Mindset

- Traders with this mindset recognize the importance of education and continuous improvement. They view losses as valuable learning experiences and are committed to refining their skills.

- Example: Emily, a beginner in options trading, starts with a small account and a commitment to learning. She reads books, takes online courses, and keeps a trading journal. When she faces losses, she reviews her journal to identify areas for improvement. Over time, Emily's disciplined approach pays off, and she becomes a proficient options trader.

The Overconfident Trader Mindset

- Overconfident traders believe they possess superior knowledge and skills, often leading to excessive risk-taking and impulsive decisions.

- Example: Robert, who has experienced initial success in options trading, becomes overconfident in his abilities. He starts leveraging his positions heavily, convinced that he can't go wrong. When the market takes an unexpected turn, his portfolio faces significant losses, highlighting the perils of unchecked overconfidence.

The Pragmatic and Goal-Oriented Mindset

- Traders with a pragmatic mindset set clear goals, create structured trading plans, and adhere to predefined strategies. They prioritize consistent, disciplined trading over impulsive actions.

- Example: Lisa sets specific goals for her options trading, such as a monthly income target. She creates a trading plan that includes entry and exit criteria, risk management rules, and position sizing guidelines. By sticking to her plan and adjusting when necessary, Lisa achieves her trading goals over time.

The Fearful and Risk-Averse Mindset

- Traders with a fearful mindset are overly concerned about losses. They may hesitate to take calculated risks, missing out on potential opportunities.

- Example: David, after experiencing a few small losses in options trading, becomes extremely risk-averse. He avoids taking positions that carry any significant risk, missing out on potentially profitable trades. His fear of losses prevents him from fully capitalizing on his trading strategies.

The Trend-Follower Mindset

- Trend-following traders focus on identifying and capitalizing on market trends. They aim to ride momentum and may use technical analysis extensively.

- Example: Maria, a trend-follower, uses moving averages and trend indicators to identify stocks with strong upward momentum. She enters options trades aligned with the prevailing trend, aiming for profits as long as the trend persists. This strategy can be profitable during strong, sustained trends.

The Options Enthusiast Mindset

- Traders with this mindset are genuinely passionate about options trading. They are eager to learn and stay informed about various options strategies and market conditions.

- Example: Alex has a deep interest in options trading and regularly attends webinars, reads options-related books, and participates in trading forums. He enjoys the process of analyzing different strategies and adjusting his approach based on changing market conditions. His enthusiasm fuels his dedication and ongoing success in options trading.

The Diverse and Adaptive Mindset

- Traders with a diverse and adaptive mindset possess a wide range of skills and are willing to adapt to different market conditions. They recognize that flexibility is key to long-term success.

- Example: Mark, a seasoned options trader, is adept at various strategies, including covered calls, straddles, and iron condors. He adjusts his approach based on market volatility, economic events, and changing trends. Mark's ability to adapt allows him to consistently navigate diverse market conditions successfully.

The Intelligent but Undisciplined Mindset

- Traders with this mindset possess a high level of intelligence and a deep understanding of how options trading and finance work. They may be well-versed in complex strategies and market dynamics, but their Achilles' heel is their inability to consistently follow their own well-reasoned plans and rules.

- Example: Meet Jason, a trader with an impressive background in finance and a knack for analyzing market data. He often formulates intricate options strategies with great precision, anticipating market movements accurately. However, Jason's undisciplined approach leads him to deviate from his plans, abandon risk management principles, and occasionally succumb to impulsive trades. Despite his intelligence, his inability to maintain discipline hinders him from realizing his full trading potential.

The "Intelligent but Undisciplined Mindset" underscores the importance of not only having knowledge but also having the discipline to execute well-thought-out trading strategies consistently. Traders with this mindset may find that improving their self-discipline becomes a critical factor in achieving their desired trading success.

The Derivatives Skeptic Mindset

- Traders with this mindset harbor strong reservations or doubts about the value and legitimacy of derivatives, including options. They firmly believe that traditional investing, such as buying and holding stocks or bonds, is the only valid approach to building wealth. They not only abstain from trading derivatives themselves but also actively caution others against exploring this financial realm.

- Example: Meet Susan, a seasoned investor who has built a successful portfolio through long-term investments in stocks and bonds. Susan is deeply skeptical of derivatives, particularly options, viewing them as speculative and overly complex. She avoids options trading entirely and often advises friends and family against venturing into derivatives, warning them of potential risks. While Susan's conservative approach has served her well, it also means she misses out on opportunities that derivatives trading can offer, such as income generation and risk management.

The "Derivatives Skeptic Mindset" reflects a cautious and risk-averse approach to investing, rooted in a belief that traditional methods are inherently safer. Traders with this mindset may prioritize capital preservation and simplicity but could potentially miss out on the benefits of derivatives, which can be valuable tools when used prudently and with proper risk management.

The Buyer Mindset

- Traders with the Buyer Mindset tend to favor buying options, such as call options for bullish bets or put options for bearish bets. They believe that this approach provides them with unlimited profit potential while limiting their risk to the premium paid for the options contract. This mindset can be influenced by the desire for quick and substantial gains without the complexities of selling options or managing positions.

- Example: Alex is a trader with a strong Buyer Mindset. He frequently scans the market for stocks with high volatility and buys out-of-the-money call options with the expectation of a rapid price increase. He sees buying options as the most straightforward way to profit from market movements. While he occasionally experiences significant gains, he also faces the risk of losing the entire premium paid if the market doesn't move in his favor.

The Seller Mindset

-Traders with the Seller Mindset are inclined to sell options contracts, such as covered calls, cash-secured puts, or credit spreads. They prioritize generating income from collecting premiums and believe that they can profit consistently by managing their positions and leveraging the time decay of options. This mindset is rooted in the idea that a high percentage of options expire worthless, allowing sellers to keep the premiums they've received.

-Example: Emily has a strong Seller Mindset in her options trading strategy. She regularly sells covered calls on stocks she owns to generate additional income. Emily understands that while this strategy limits her potential for unlimited gains, it offers a steady stream of premiums. She appreciates the probabilities working in her favor, as most options contracts expire without the need for further action, allowing her to keep the premiums and continue generating income.

The Perfect Mindset

- Some traders believe in the existence of a "perfect" mindset—a one-size-fits-all approach that guarantees success in options trading. They often seek the holy grail of trading strategies, believing that once found, it will eliminate all risks and secure unending profits. However, the reality is quite different.

In truth, there is no universally perfect mindset in options trading. Human beings are complex creatures, subject to emotions, biases, and unique life circumstances. What works impeccably for one trader may be a recipe for failure for another.

The perfect mindset, therefore, lies in the acknowledgment that perfection doesn't exist in trading. Instead, it revolves around self-awareness, recognizing one's individual risk tolerance, emotional strengths and weaknesses, and aligning trading strategies accordingly.

- Example: Consider James, who fervently believed that adopting a specific trading strategy he read about online would lead to unblemished success. He disregarded his own risk tolerance and personality traits. After a series of losses and emotional turmoil, James realized that a perfect, one-size-fits-all mindset was a myth. He began to focus on understanding his unique strengths, weaknesses, and emotional triggers. James then crafted a trading approach tailored to his individual profile, which ultimately led to more consistent and profitable trading.

In essence, the "Perfect Mindset" is not about seeking a universal solution but rather understanding oneself and adapting trading strategies accordingly. It's the recognition that embracing our humanity, with all its intricacies and idiosyncrasies, is the true path to success in options trading.

These diverse mindsets highlight the range of approaches and attitudes that traders bring to options trading. Recognizing their own mindset and understanding its implications can empower traders to make more informed decisions and adapt their strategies to align with their trading goals and risk tolerance.

While these mindsets provide valuable perspectives, it's important to understand that they represent only a portion of the intricate tapestry of trader psychology. The human mind, with its adaptability and complexity, defies easy categorization. While many traders may resonate with these profiles, it's essential to remember that they are not exhaustive.

The Essence of Emotional Intelligence
In the dynamic world of options trading, the mastery of emotional intelligence isn't merely a desirable attribute; it's often the definitive factor that separates success from failure. Emotional intelligence, commonly referred to as EQ (Emotional Quotient), is the profound ability to not only recognize and understand emotions but also to manage and utilize them effectively. This vital skill holds the power to profoundly influence decision-making, risk management, and overall performance within the high-stakes arena of financial markets.

Emotional intelligence constitutes a multifaceted spectrum of capabilities, and within the context of options trading, it plays a crucial, multidimensional role. Let's embark on an exploration of the core components of emotional intelligence and delve into how they weave into the fabric of trading.

Self-Awareness: The Foundation of Emotional Intelligence

At its core, emotional intelligence finds its roots in self-awareness. This cornerstone involves the ability to recognize your emotions as they emerge, understand their origins, and fathom how they shape your thoughts and actions. In the realm of options trading, self-awareness entails staying in tune with your emotional responses to market shifts, trade outcomes, and personal biases.

Example: Picture this scenario: You've just executed a promising options trade, and the market takes an unexpected turn, resulting in a substantial loss. Self-awareness empowers you to acknowledge the frustration and disappointment you're feeling without letting it cloud your judgment. This, in turn, allows you to objectively evaluate the trade and decide on the next steps.

Practical Exercise: To deepen your self-awareness, keep a trading journal where you meticulously document your emotional responses to each trade. Reflect on how these emotions impact your decision-making and uncover patterns over time. This exercise will not only enhance your self-awareness but also enable you to anticipate emotional responses in future trades.

Self-Regulation: Managing Your Emotional Responses

Once you've developed self-awareness, the next stride involves self-regulation, which entails effectively managing your emotional reactions. In the context of options trading, this skill is paramount for thwarting impulsive decisions driven by fear, greed, or frustration.

Example: Amidst a volatile market, fear may surge, and the impulse to exit a trade prematurely can be overwhelming. Self-regulation equips you with the ability to pause, assess the situation impartially, and make decisions grounded in your trading strategy rather than emotional reactions.

Practical Exercise: Enhance your self-regulation by incorporating mindfulness meditation into your daily routine. Meditation nurtures the capacity to remain composed and centered even in the throes of stressful trading situations, facilitating more judicious decision-making.

Empathy: Understanding Market Sentiment

Empathy, the ability to comprehend and relate to the emotions of others, plays a pivotal role in trading. In this context, empathy involves considering market sentiment and empathizing with the emotional reactions of fellow market participants, which can yield valuable insights.

Example: If you discern widespread panic within the market due to a macroeconomic event, empathizing with the collective fear can empower you to anticipate market shifts and strategically position your trades.

Practical Exercise: Engage in discussions and forums with fellow traders to gain insight into their emotional perspectives. This practice will amplify your empathy and equip you to better anticipate market sentiment.

Social Skills: Effective Communication and Collaboration

Effective communication and interpersonal skills are indispensable in options trading. Building relationships with other traders, brokers, and financial experts can provide invaluable insights and support when navigating the markets.

Example: Networking with seasoned traders may open doors to mentorship opportunities, where you can glean wisdom from their experiences with emotional intelligence and trading.

Practical Exercise: Attend trading seminars, webinars, or local trading groups to refine your social skills and expand your network within the trading community.

Motivation: Sustaining Your Trading Goals

Within the domain of emotional intelligence, motivation refers to the drive to remain committed to your trading objectives despite challenges and setbacks. It's the propelling force that keeps you engaged and resilient when confronted with adversity.

Example: Even after a series of setbacks, a trader fueled by high motivation remains unwavering in their resolve to refine their strategies and enhance their emotional intelligence, ultimately striving to attain their financial aspirations.

Practical Exercise: Set clear, achievable trading goals and routinely revisit them to stay motivated. Break down overarching objectives into smaller, manageable milestones to sustain a sense of progress.

As we delve into the intricacies of emotional intelligence, it's essential to acknowledge the most common emotions that traders encounter in the exciting yet volatile world of options trading. Fear, greed, hope/overconfidence, and regret are emotions that often sway trading decisions. We will delve into each of these emotions in detail in their respective chapters, exploring their origins, impact on trading outcomes, and effective strategies for managing them.

Harnessing Emotional Intelligence in Trading

Now that we've explored the components of emotional intelligence, let's discuss how to apply them in the world of options trading.

Recognizing Emotional Triggers: As a trader, identifying specific situations or market conditions that trigger emotional responses is crucial. It might be a losing streak, a sudden market crash, or even the fear of missing out on a lucrative opportunity. Once you identify these triggers, you can prepare strategies to manage your emotions when they arise.

Implementing a Trading Plan: A well-defined trading plan serves as a road map for navigating the markets. It outlines entry and exit strategies, risk management rules, and criteria for trade execution. When emotions threaten to sway your decisions, adhering to your trading plan can provide a structured and rational approach.

Practicing Patience: Emotional intelligence fosters patience, a virtue often underestimated in options trading. Patience allows you to wait for optimal entry points and avoid impulsive decisions.

Remember that not every market movement requires immediate action.

Embracing Losses: Emotional intelligence helps you accept losses as part of the trading journey. Instead of dwelling on past mistakes, you learn from them and apply those lessons to future trades. This resilience is essential for long-term success.

Seeking Support: Don't hesitate to seek support from trading communities, mentors and peers. Discussing your experiences and emotions with others can provide valuable perspective and coping strategies.

Emotional intelligence is the linchpin of success in options trading. By cultivating self-awareness, self-regulation, empathy, social skills, and motivation, traders can enhance their decision-making, adapt to market conditions, and navigate the complexities of the financial markets with resilience and wisdom. Remember, the journey to mastering emotional intelligence is ongoing, but the rewards in terms of trading success and personal growth are immeasurable.

2. Neurochemistry and Options Trading: The Inner Workings of the Trader's Brain

Understanding the neurochemistry of traders is vital in the context of options trading. Neurochemicals profoundly affect traders' emotions, behaviors, and decision-making. This chapter delves into the role of neurochemicals in shaping trading psychology and offers insights to enhance trading performance. Traders operate in a complex landscape of market data and financial variables while managing their emotional responses to gains and losses. Neurochemicals are the biochemical messengers behind these responses. In this chapter, we explore the roles of key neurotransmitters like dopamine, serotonin, and cortisol in influencing traders' emotional states and decisions. We also discuss strategies to harness neurochemistry for improved trading outcomes.

Neurochemical Fundamentals

Neurochemicals are chemical compounds within the brain and nervous system that serve as messengers, facilitating communication between nerve cells, or neurons. These compounds include neurotransmitters and hormones, and they play a vital role in regulating various brain functions, emotions, and behaviors. Neurochemicals influence mood, cognition, stress responses, and decision-making processes. Below are some of the key neurochemicals that impacts trading significantly.

Dopamine: Known as the "feel-good" neurotransmitter, dopamine is associated with reward and pleasure. In trading, dopamine surges when a trader makes a profitable trade, creating a sense of euphoria. Conversely, losses can lead to a drop in dopamine levels, causing frustration and disappointment.

Serotonin: Often referred to as the "feel-well" neurotransmitter, serotonin contributes to feelings of well-being and confidence.

Traders with balanced serotonin levels tend to make more rational decisions, while imbalances can lead to impulsive actions.

Cortisol: The "stress hormone," cortisol, rises in response to stress and perceived threats. In trading, excessive cortisol can cloud judgment, trigger fear-based decisions, and impair cognitive functions.

Adrenaline (Norepinephrine): This neurotransmitter, often referred to as adrenaline, plays a crucial role in the "fight or flight" response. Elevated adrenaline levels can lead to heightened alertness, increased heart rate, and impulsive trading decisions driven by fear and panic during market volatility.

Endorphins: Endorphins act as natural painkillers and mood elevators. In trading, they can contribute to a sense of euphoria after a winning streak, potentially leading to overconfidence and risky behavior.

Oxytocin: Often called the "love hormone" or "bonding hormone," oxytocin fosters trust and social connections. In trading, positive social interactions with fellow traders can trigger oxytocin release, promoting a sense of community and collaboration.

Acetylcholine: Acetylcholine plays a role in learning, memory, and cognitive functions. Balanced acetylcholine levels support sound decision-making and adaptability in changing market conditions.

Glutamate: As an excitatory neurotransmitter, glutamate plays a role in learning, memory, and cognitive functions. Imbalances can lead to impulsive trading and difficulty in controlling emotions, as it can amplify reactions to market events.

Exploring Emotions via Neurochemicals

In the world of options trading, emotions play a pivotal role in shaping traders' decisions, behaviors, and outcomes. These emotions are not just abstract feelings but are deeply intertwined with the brain's chemistry, governed by a complex web of neurochemicals. Understanding how specific neurochemicals can trigger a range of emotions is crucial for traders seeking to navigate the tumultuous seas of the financial markets.

Fear and Cortisol:

Fear is a pervasive emotion in trading, often driven by the release of cortisol, the body's primary stress hormone. When traders encounter perceived threats, such as significant market downturns or potential losses, cortisol levels surge. This heightened state of alertness can lead to irrational decisions, such as hastily exiting a position or avoiding potentially profitable opportunities out of fear.

Greed and Dopamine:

Greed, the insatiable desire for financial gain, is closely associated with the release of dopamine, a neurotransmitter that plays a central role in the brain's reward system. Profits generated from successful trades can trigger dopamine surges, creating a sense of euphoria and an insatiable appetite for greater gains. Unchecked greed can lead to overtrading, excessive risk-taking, and ultimately, significant losses.

Hope and Endorphins:

Hope is a powerful and motivating emotion in trading, often linked to the release of endorphins, the body's natural feel-good chemicals. Anticipating a profitable trade can induce the release of endorphins, fostering feelings of optimism and well-being. However, unwarranted hope can lead traders to stubbornly hold onto losing positions, driven by the desire to experience the positive emotions associated with success.

Patience and Serotonin:

Patience, a virtue prized by successful traders, is associated with serotonin, a neurotransmitter responsible for mood stability and overall well-being. Maintaining balanced serotonin levels can help traders make more rational and patient decisions. Serotonin fosters a sense of confidence and emotional stability, qualities essential for patiently awaiting the right trading opportunities and effectively managing open positions.

Regret and Norepinephrine (Adrenaline):

Regret is a common emotion in trading, often triggered by norepinephrine (also known as adrenaline). Traders may experience regret when reflecting on their decisions, especially after incurring losses. Elevated norepinephrine levels can lead to heightened alertness, impulsivity, and a strong desire to rectify past mistakes. It's essential for traders to manage regret effectively to avoid making impulsive decisions that can exacerbate losses.

Excitement and Glutamate:

Excitement is an emotion that traders often experience during moments of market volatility or when witnessing significant price movements. This emotion is linked to glutamate, a neurotransmitter that plays a key role in neural communication. Glutamate can intensify emotional responses, leading traders to make impulsive decisions driven by excitement rather than a well-thought-out strategy.

Now that we have delved into the realm of neurochemicals and their intricate connection with various emotions, we've unlocked a profound insight into our own moods. This understanding empowers us to recognize potential chemical imbalances that may impact our decision-making and emotional well-being. In the upcoming section, we will explore effective strategies to address and manage these imbalances, equipping us with valuable tools to navigate the complex world of options trading with greater emotional intelligence and resilience

Nurturing a Balanced Neurochemical Environment

In this section, we delve into practical strategies for restoring neurochemical balance when imbalances occur. Each neurochemical plays a vital role in influencing our emotions and behaviors, and understanding how to bring them back to normal levels can be a valuable tool for traders.

1. Dopamine Regulation: If you find yourself in a constant cycle of seeking quick trading thrills and impulsive decisions (linked to excessive dopamine), consider strategies to regulate it. Engage in activities that provide delayed gratification, such as long-term investing or setting clear trading goals with gradual rewards.

2. Serotonin Stabilization: For traders struggling with anxiety and self-doubt (often associated with low serotonin levels), focus on activities that naturally boost serotonin production. Regular exercise, exposure to sunlight, and maintaining a balanced diet with foods rich in tryptophan (an amino acid precursor to serotonin) can help.

3. Cortisol Reduction: High stress levels and cortisol imbalances can be detrimental to trading success. Incorporate stress-reduction techniques such as meditation, yoga, or deep breathing exercises into your daily routine. Prioritize quality sleep and avoid excessive caffeine intake, which can exacerbate cortisol levels.

4. Oxytocin Enhancement: If you're facing challenges related to trust, bonding, and social connections (areas where oxytocin plays a key role), consider strengthening your interpersonal relationships. Spend quality time with loved ones, engage in acts of kindness, or join trading communities to foster a sense of belonging.

5. Endorphin Release: To counteract periods of emotional distress, activate your body's endorphin release system. Engage in regular physical activity, whether it's jogging, dancing, or even laughter-

inducing activities. These activities can naturally boost endorphin levels, promoting a sense of well-being.

6. Glutamate Balance: Elevated glutamate levels can contribute to anxiety and overthinking. Adopt a balanced diet rich in magnesium, vitamin B6, and antioxidants, as they are known to help regulate glutamate levels. Consider consulting with a healthcare professional for guidance on dietary supplements.

7. Norepinephrine Management: If excessive norepinephrine is leading to heightened stress and emotional volatility, implement stress-management strategies. Regular exercise, deep breathing exercises, and progressive muscle relaxation can help manage norepinephrine levels.

Traders often underestimate the profound impact of neurochemicals on their trading success. While technical analysis skills, market knowledge, and product expertise are undeniably crucial, neglecting the role of neurochemistry can hinder their overall performance. It's a common misconception that trading is solely a cognitive endeavor, and factors like sleep quality, nutrition, and emotional well-being hold no relevance in the trading equation. However, as we delve into case studies in the next section of this chapter, we'll uncover case studies that illuminate the significant influence of neurochemical balance on traders' decision-making, emotional resilience, and long-term success in the complex world of options trading.

Neurochemistry: Trader Case Studies

Trader Story 1: Breaking the Midnight Cycle

Hussain, an avid Indian options trader, possessed a relentless dedication to the market that knew no bounds. His trading routine was marred by a habit that had slowly crept into his life over the years—an obsession with the SGX NIFTY.

Each night, as the clock ticked away, Hussain's anticipation grew. Unable to resist the urge, he would set alarms to wake him up at the slightest movement in the SGX NIFTY. Whether it was midnight or the wee hours of dawn, Hussain would spring out of bed to check the market.

This relentless cycle of sleep deprivation and constant vigilance was taking a toll on Hussain's neurochemistry. His dopamine levels were on a rollercoaster ride, surging with every promising sign in the SGX NIFTY and plummeting with each unfavorable fluctuation. Cortisol, the stress hormone, ran rampant, contributing to his sleeplessness and increasing his anxiety.

Over time, Hussain began to notice the adverse effects of his sleep-deprived, neurochemically imbalanced state. He was increasingly prone to impulsive trading decisions and found it challenging to maintain patience during market turbulence. The toll on his mental and emotional well-being was undeniable.

One day, after enduring yet another sleepless night, Hussain decided it was time for a change. He reached out to a trading coach who specialized in addressing unhealthy trading habits and their impact on traders' neurochemistry.

Under the guidance of the coach, Hussain gradually reformed his routine. He learned to set boundaries, allowing himself a restful night's sleep without constantly checking the SGX NIFTY. Meditation and relaxation techniques became a part of his daily regimen, helping to balance his neurochemicals and reduce stress.

As Hussain adopted a more balanced approach to trading and self-care, his neurochemical environment began to stabilize. His decision-making improved, and he felt more in control of his emotions during trading. While breaking the midnight cycle was not easy, it was essential for Hussain's long-term success.

Hussain's story underscores the critical connection between healthy sleep patterns, neurochemical balance, and effective trading. It serves as a valuable reminder that nurturing one's neurochemical environment is a key aspect of achieving sustainable success in the challenging world of options trading.

Trader Story 2: Love and Trading: A Neurochemical Journey

Meet Ryan, an options trader who wore his heart on his sleeve, both in love and in trading. Ryan's relationship was a rollercoaster, filled with moments of bliss and intense arguments. When his love life was in harmony, he was on top of the world, his serotonin levels soaring. However, when conflicts arose with his partner, the emotional turbulence sent his cortisol levels skyrocketing, plunging him into deep misery.

This tumultuous relationship had a profound impact on Ryan's neurochemistry, which in turn influenced his trading decisions. During the highs of his love life, when his serotonin levels were abundant, he felt invincible and took more significant risks in the options market. He often made impulsive trades and threw caution to the wind.

However, when he experienced conflicts or fights with his partner, his cortisol levels surged, clouding his judgment and decision-making abilities. Ryan would become paralyzed by stress and anxiety, unable to focus on his trading strategies. He often exited positions prematurely or entered high-stress trades, hoping to compensate for the emotional turmoil he was experiencing in his personal life.

One day, after a particularly heated argument with his partner, Ryan realized that his turbulent love life was directly affecting his trading performance and overall well-being. He decided it was time to take control of his emotions and neurochemistry.

Ryan began seeking therapy to address the underlying issues in his relationship. Through counseling, he learned strategies to manage conflict and reduce stress. He also adopted mindfulness practices and meditation to balance his neurochemicals and calm his mind.

As he made progress in his personal life, Ryan noticed a significant improvement in his trading. His decision-making became more rational, and he could withstand market fluctuations with resilience. By nurturing a healthier neurochemical environment, he was better equipped to navigate the challenges of options trading.

Ryan's story serves as a testament to the intricate relationship between personal life, emotions, and trading. It underscores the importance of recognizing how neurochemical imbalances can impact trading decisions and the value of taking steps to maintain emotional well-being both inside and outside the trading room.

Trader Story 3: Dopamine Overload to Trading Triumph

Daniel, an options trader with dreams of financial success, was unknowingly sabotaging his trading career with a series of detrimental habits. His days were consumed by mindless scrolling through short videos, endless hours on social media, and a regular diet filled with junk food. These habits provided him with quick dopamine hits, but they came at a steep price.

As the weeks turned into months, Daniel noticed the toll these habits were taking on his neurochemistry. He became irritable, impatient, and easily distracted. His once-sharp focus on the markets was replaced by a constant craving for instant gratification.

During trading hours, Daniel's impulsive decisions led to mounting losses. Instead of following his well-researched strategies, he found himself chasing after quick wins, driven by the same dopamine cravings that fueled his unhealthy habits.

One day, as he watched his trading account balance plunge to a new low, Daniel had a sobering realization. His pursuit of cheap dopamine boosts was not only affecting his trading but also his overall well-being. He knew that if he wanted to succeed in options trading, he had to break free from the grip of these habits.

With determination, Daniel began to make positive changes in his life. He reduced his screen time significantly, limiting his exposure to the endless scroll of social media and addictive short videos. Instead, he used that time to engage in physical activities, taking long walks and enjoying the outdoors.

His diet underwent a transformation as well. Daniel swapped out junk food for nutritious options, providing his brain with the essential nutrients it needed to function at its best. He also integrated mindfulness and meditation into his daily routine, helping him regain control over his impulses.

As the weeks passed, Daniel's neurochemistry started to rebalance itself. His cravings for instant gratification began to fade, and his mental clarity improved. He regained his ability to focus on market analysis, sticking to his trading plan with discipline.

With newfound clarity and control over his emotions, Daniel's trading performance took a positive turn. He started to see consistent profits, and his losses became less frequent. The discipline he had longed for was now a reality.

Daniel's journey from the clutches of dopamine-driven habits to trading success serves as a powerful reminder of the impact of neurochemistry on trading performance. It showcases the transformative potential of breaking free from unhealthy habits and nurturing a balanced neurochemical environment for trading excellence.

3: Greed and Its Consequences: Finding Balance in Risk-Taking

The emotion of greed can be both enticing and perilous. It is a powerful force that can lead traders to make impulsive decisions, overexpose themselves to risk, and ultimately undermine their financial goals. In this chapter, we will delve deep into the concept of greed in options trading, exploring its nature, triggers, consequences, and most importantly, strategies to effectively manage this emotion.

Understanding Greed in Options Trading
What is Greed in Options Trading?

Greed, within the context of options trading, is an intense desire for excessive gains and a relentless pursuit of profits. It often emerges when traders become fixated on the potential for enormous returns and disregard the associated risks. This emotion can lead to reckless decision-making and, ironically, result in significant losses.

Why Do Traders Feel Greed?

The roots of greed in options trading are multifaceted and can be attributed to several factors:

1. Profit Aspirations: Traders enter the market with the aspiration of making substantial profits. The prospect of realizing significant gains can trigger greed when those profits seem within reach.

2. Fear of Missing Out (FOMO): Traders often fear missing out on lucrative opportunities, especially during periods of rapid market growth. This fear can lead to impulsive actions driven by greed.

3. Past Successes: Previous profitable trades can inflate one's ego and fuel overconfidence, making traders more susceptible to greed.

4. Peer Pressure: Observing others making substantial gains can invoke a sense of competitiveness and the desire to replicate their success.

5. Market Hype: Bull markets and hot investment trends can create a euphoric atmosphere that encourages excessive risk-taking and greed.

Common Triggers for Greed

Greed tends to rear its head under certain conditions:

1. Bull Markets: During strong upward market trends, traders may feel the urge to maximize profits, even if it means taking on excessive risk.

2. Sudden Price Surges: When an asset's price experiences a rapid and unexpected increase, traders might become greedy and invest without adequate due diligence.

3. Herd Mentality: Following the crowd, especially during speculative bubbles, can lead to greed as traders seek to capitalize on the momentum.

4. Unrealistic Expectations: Greed can be fueled by the unrealistic belief that profits will continue to grow indefinitely.

Impact of Greed on Options Trading

While greed can be tempting, it can have detrimental effects on options trading:

1. Overtrading: Greedy traders may engage in excessive buying and selling, resulting in high transaction costs and reduced profitability.

2. Lack of Discipline: Greed can cloud judgment and lead to impulsive decisions, causing traders to deviate from their well-thought-out trading plans.

3. Increased Risk Exposure: The pursuit of high profits often involves taking on higher levels of risk, potentially leading to substantial losses.

4. Emotional Rollercoaster: Traders driven by greed may experience extreme emotional highs and lows, which can be mentally exhausting.

Managing Greed in Options Trading

Effectively managing greed is essential for sustainable options trading success. Here are strategies and techniques to keep greed in check:

1. Set Realistic Goals:

Define clear, achievable profit targets for each trade and avoid becoming overly fixated on unrealistic gains.

2. Stick to a Trading Plan:

Develop a well-defined trading plan that includes entry and exit strategies. Adhere to your plan, regardless of the allure of higher profits.

3. Implement Risk Management:

Use stop-loss orders and position sizing techniques to limit potential losses. A disciplined approach to risk management can mitigate the impact of greed.

4. Diversify Your Portfolio:

Spread your investments across different assets and strategies to reduce overconcentration and the temptation to chase extraordinary gains.

5. Practice Patience:

Understand that not every market movement requires immediate action. Patience can help you avoid impulsive decisions driven by greed.

6. Maintain Emotional Awareness:

Continuously monitor your emotions during trading. If you sense greed creeping in, step back and reevaluate your decisions.

Practical Exercises to Overcome Greed

Exercise 1: Greed Journal

Create a "Greed Journal" where you document instances of greed in your trading decisions. Include details such as the assets involved, your emotions, and the outcomes. Review this journal regularly to identify patterns.

Exercise 2: Visualization Techniques

Practice visualization exercises where you imagine scenarios where you resist the temptation of greed and make rational, disciplined decisions. Visualization can help train your mind to stay focused on your trading plan.

Greed: Trader Case Studies
Trader Story 1: The Greed-Driven Gamble

Mark, an experienced options trader, had a successful track record built over several years. During a particularly bullish market phase, he noticed an emerging trend in a tech stock that seemed like a surefire opportunity for substantial profits. However, as the stock price soared, greed got the better of him.

The Greedy Move: Ignoring his usual risk management rules, Mark invested a significant portion of his portfolio in short-term call options for the tech stock. He believed that the stock's relentless ascent would continue without end.

The Consequence: Unfortunately, the market proved unpredictable. A sudden market correction led to a sharp decline in the tech stock's price. Mark's portfolio suffered significant losses, wiping out months of gains.

The Redemption: Mark, realizing the error of his ways, took a step back and assessed the situation. He acknowledged that greed had clouded his judgment. To recover his losses, he reframed his strategy, focusing on a more balanced and diversified portfolio. Over time, he managed to regain his losses and learned the importance of disciplined trading.

Trader Story 2: A Lesson in Overtrading

Sarah, a relatively new options trader, had experienced initial success with a series of profitable trades. As her confidence grew, she became increasingly eager to capitalize on every market opportunity that came her way.

The Greedy Move: Sarah started overtrading, frequently entering and exiting positions in pursuit of quick profits. Her fear of missing out (FOMO) drove her to make impulsive trades without proper analysis.

The Consequence: Over time, her trading account dwindled due to excessive transaction costs, and her emotional well-being suffered. Her rapid-fire approach to trading resulted in inconsistent and unpredictable outcomes.

The Redemption: Realizing that her greed-driven overtrading was undermining her goals, Sarah decided to take a step back. She sought education and mentorship to refine her trading strategy. With patience, discipline, and a newfound commitment to risk management, she managed to regain her confidence and rebuild her trading account.

Trader Story 3: Chasing the Illusive Dream

John, an options trader with aspirations of substantial wealth, was constantly on the lookout for the next big opportunity. He had experienced some significant gains in the past, which fueled his desire for more.

The Greedy Move: John became fixated on speculative stocks and options with high potential returns. He consistently invested large portions of his capital in these high-risk assets, hoping for extraordinary profits.

The Consequence: While he occasionally enjoyed spectacular gains, they were often overshadowed by even larger losses. His inability to control his appetite for high-risk trades resulted in a rollercoaster of financial ups and downs.

The Redemption: Recognizing the destructive cycle of greed, John decided to reevaluate his approach. He diversified his portfolio, incorporating more conservative investments while allocating a smaller portion of his capital to high-risk trades. Over time, this balanced approach provided steadier returns and reduced the emotional stress associated with excessive greed.

Trader Story 4: The Costly Hillside Trade

Ganesh, an options trader with an insatiable appetite for profit, had been eagerly anticipating a long-planned picnic to the hillside with his family. Aware that the remote location offered no network connectivity, he decided to take an ambitious trade on a popular stock just before departing.

The Greedy Move: Moments before heading into the hills, Ganesh entered a high-stakes trade with a substantial position size, convinced that he could quickly profit and cover his picnic expenses. He couldn't resist the allure of potential gains.

The Consequence: As expected, the moment Ganesh ventured into the hilly terrain, his network connection vanished. Unbeknownst to him, the market took an unpredictable turn. When he finally regained connectivity hours later, he was met with a staggering loss.

The Redemption: The shock of his impulsive decision hit Ganesh hard. He realized that his greed had cost him not only financially but also the quality time he had planned to spend with his family. Determined to make amends, he reassessed his trading behavior.

Ganesh decided to adopt a more disciplined approach. He started by setting strict trading rules, which included not trading during family outings or vacations. He committed to separating his trading and personal life, allowing him to focus fully on each when the time was right.

Over time, Ganesh's trading improved. He learned to curb his impulsive greed and to prioritize his family and personal well-being over reckless trades. His newfound discipline not only protected his capital but also allowed him to fully enjoy his future picnics and vacations with his loved ones. Ganesh's story serves as a valuable lesson in the importance of setting boundaries and avoiding the pitfalls of greed in options trading.

Trader Story 5: The Forgotten Trade

Venkat, a dedicated professional and an aspiring options trader, had a demanding job that required his full attention during office hours. However, he couldn't resist the temptation of making quick profits in the financial markets, even while commuting to his workplace.

The Greedy Move: One fateful morning, Venkat decided to take a significant position in Bank Nifty options just before he left for the office. He believed he could easily manage the trade while juggling his work responsibilities, fueled by the allure of potential gains.

The Consequence: As soon as Venkat reached his office, his day was consumed by a series of unexpected meetings and urgent tasks. He completely forgot about the trade he had initiated earlier in the morning. It wasn't until much later in the day, after the markets had closed, that he remembered the trade. When he checked his trading account, he was greeted by substantial losses.

The Redemption: Shocked and disappointed by his own negligence, Venkat realized that his greed and inability to resist trading during work hours had cost him dearly. Determined to rectify his mistake, he took decisive action.

Venkat decided to set strict boundaries between his trading and professional life. He established a clear trading schedule, reserving only non-office hours for trading activities. He also made use of order types that automatically managed his positions, such as stop-loss orders, which could have protected him from significant losses in the forgotten trade.

Over time, Venkat's discipline and newfound commitment to his professional responsibilities and trading paid off. He not only avoided similar trading mishaps but also saw improved results in his options trading. The lesson he learned was invaluable: greed and neglecting responsibilities can lead to costly mistakes, but discipline and boundaries can lead to trading success and a balanced life.

Venkat's story serves as a reminder that effective time management and a disciplined approach to trading can help traders overcome the lure of greed and prevent avoidable losses.

These trader stories vividly illustrate the pitfalls of unchecked greed in options trading. Greed can drive traders to make impulsive decisions, ignore risk management principles, and chase unrealistic dreams of profit. However, each of these traders ultimately recognized the adverse impact of greed on their trading and took steps to rectify their mistakes.

The key takeaway from these stories is that it's possible to recover from the consequences of greed by adopting a disciplined and balanced approach to trading. Traders can learn from their mistakes, seek education and mentorship, and implement strategies to manage their emotions effectively. In the following chapters, we will explore more emotions and provide guidance on achieving emotional balance for successful options trading.

4: The Fear Factor: Overcoming Anxiety in Options Trading

Fear is an emotion that frequently takes center stage. It's a pervasive and often overwhelming feeling that can profoundly affect traders' decisions and, subsequently, their success in the financial markets. In this chapter, we will explore fear in options trading comprehensively—what it is, why traders experience it, when it typically arises, the profound impact it has on options trading, and, most importantly, effective strategies and practical exercises to conquer this formidable emotion.

Understanding Fear in Options Trading
What is Fear in Options Trading?

Fear, in the context of options trading, is an intense emotional response to the perception of risk and uncertainty. It's the apprehension that accompanies the possibility of losing capital or facing adverse market conditions. Fear often manifests as anxiety, panic, or a sense of impending doom, and it can significantly influence traders' decisions.

Why Do Traders Feel Fear?

The experience of fear in options trading can be attributed to several factors:

1. Loss Aversion: Human nature is inherently averse to losses. Traders are no exception, and the fear of losing capital can be a powerful motivator for anxious feelings.

2. Uncertainty: The financial markets are inherently uncertain and unpredictable. This ambiguity can trigger fear as traders grapple with the vast unknown and the potential consequences for their investments.

3. Psychological Impact of Losses: Past trading losses can leave emotional scars, leading to a fear of repeating those mistakes and the associated pain.

4. Pressure to Perform: The pressure to meet financial goals and expectations can intensify fear, especially when trading with significant capital.

5. Market Volatility: Volatile market conditions can exacerbate fear. Rapid price fluctuations and unpredictable market behavior can be deeply unsettling, even for experienced traders.

Common Triggers for Fear
Fear typically arises under specific conditions:

1. Market Turbulence: Sudden market downturns or extreme volatility can trigger fear as traders witness the rapid erosion of their portfolio values.

2. Unforeseen Events: Unexpected geopolitical events, economic crises, or corporate scandals can create an atmosphere of uncertainty, fueling fear in the markets.

3. Personal Financial Goals: Fear may intensify when traders feel that their financial well-being is at stake or when they are under pressure to achieve specific financial milestones.

4. Fear of the Unknown: The fear of not knowing what the market will do next, especially in unfamiliar or complex trading situations, can be particularly unsettling.

Impact of Fear on Options Trading
The influence of fear on options trading cannot be underestimated. It can lead to a range of detrimental effects:

1. Analysis Paralysis: Fear can lead to overthinking and indecision, causing traders to miss profitable opportunities or hesitate to take necessary actions.

2. Impulsive Reactions: In times of extreme fear, traders may make impulsive decisions, such as exiting positions prematurely or chasing losses.

3. Inconsistent Strategy: Fear can cause traders to abandon their well-thought-out trading strategies in favor of emotionally driven decisions.

4. Psychological Toll: The persistent state of fear can take a toll on traders' mental and emotional well-being, leading to stress, burnout, and reduced overall performance.

Managing Fear in Options Trading

Effectively managing fear is paramount to success in options trading. Here are strategies and techniques to help traders conquer this powerful emotion:

1. Knowledge Empowers:

Education: Deepen your understanding of options trading through research and learning. The more you know, the more confident you will become.

Risk Management: Implement rigorous risk management techniques, including setting stop-loss orders and proper position sizing. Knowing that safeguards are in place can alleviate fear.

2. Visualization and Gradual Exposure:

Visualization: Practice visualizing your trading scenarios, including both positive and negative outcomes. This exercise can help desensitize your emotional response to fear.

Gradual Exposure: Start with smaller trades and gradually increase position sizes as you gain confidence. This step-by-step approach can reduce fear associated with larger losses.

3. Mindfulness and Breathing Techniques:

Mindfulness Meditation: Incorporate mindfulness meditation into your daily routine to stay present and calm during trading. This practice can help you manage fear in high-pressure situations.

Breathing Exercises: Learn and practice deep breathing techniques to reduce anxiety and stress when fear strikes.

4. Keeping Emotions in Check:

Trading Journal: Maintain a detailed trading journal where you record your emotions, thoughts, and decisions. Reflect on these entries to identify patterns and triggers of fear.

Emotion Recognition: Train yourself to recognize fear as it arises during trading. Awareness is the first step to managing this emotion.

Practical Exercises to Overcome Fear

Exercise 1: Fear Journal

Create a "Fear Journal" alongside your trading journal. Whenever you experience fear during a trade, jot down the specific circumstances, emotions, and thoughts that triggered it. Over time, you'll gain insight into your fear patterns.

Exercise 2: Fear Exposure

Identify a trade that you find particularly fear-inducing due to its potential risk. Place this trade with a small position size, and monitor it closely. Document your emotional responses. Gradually increase the position size as you become more comfortable.

Fear: Trader Case Studies

Trader Story 1: The Paralyzed Novice

Sophia, a novice options trader, was excited to start her trading journey. However, as she placed her first few trades, she noticed that even minor market fluctuations triggered intense fear.

The Fearful Reaction: Sophia often found herself paralyzed by fear during trading. Whenever a trade moved against her, she would immediately close the position at a loss, fearing that the losses would escalate.

The Consequence: Sophia's constant fear-based decisions led to a series of losses. She was frustrated and demoralized, and her trading account was steadily dwindling.

The Redemption: Seeking guidance, Sophia joined a trading community and learned about risk management techniques. She started using stop-loss orders and proper position sizing. Over time, her fear diminished as she realized that she had control over her losses. With a disciplined approach, Sophia's trading improved, and she regained her confidence.

Trader Story 2: The Emotional Rollercoaster

David, an experienced options trader, had seen success in the past but was no stranger to fear. He had a history of making impulsive decisions when market conditions became volatile.

The Fearful Reaction: Whenever David witnessed rapid market swings, fear would grip him. His emotions oscillated between panic and irrational optimism. He frequently abandoned his trading plan, driven by fear of losing or fear of missing out.

The Consequence: David's inconsistent approach to trading resulted in erratic performance. While he had moments of brilliance, his overall profitability suffered due to his inability to manage fear effectively.

The Redemption: David recognized that his emotional rollercoaster was hindering his success. He sought out a mentor who helped him develop a more disciplined mindset. Through consistent practice of mindfulness and emotional recognition techniques, he learned to stay calm during market turbulence. Gradually, his fear-induced impulsive decisions became less frequent, and his trading became more consistent.

Trader Story 3: The Fear of Uncertainty

Alex, an options trader with a penchant for research and analysis, was well-prepared when it came to market knowledge. However, he struggled with the fear of uncertainty.

The Fearful Reaction: Alex often hesitated to enter trades due to his fear of not having all the answers. He felt the need to analyze every aspect of a potential trade, which led to missed opportunities and delayed decisions.

The Consequence: While his meticulous approach occasionally protected him from losses, it also meant missing out on profitable trades. His fear of uncertainty resulted in missed opportunities for growth.

The Redemption: Recognizing the need to overcome his fear of uncertainty, Alex implemented a trading plan that included predefined entry and exit criteria. He also started practicing visualization exercises to desensitize himself to the fear of making decisions without complete information. Over time, his fear of uncertainty diminished, and he became more decisive in his trading.

These trader stories highlight the profound impact of fear on options trading. Fear can lead to indecision, impulsive reactions, and missed opportunities. However, each of these traders recognized the detrimental effects of fear and took steps to conquer it.

Trader Story 4: The Drowning in Information

Raj, a diligent options trader, had developed a reputation for his thorough research and analysis. However, his insatiable appetite for information sometimes led him into a cycle of analysis paralysis.

The Fearful Reaction: Fearful of making a wrong decision, Raj would spend hours, sometimes days, researching and analyzing every possible aspect of a trade. He felt compelled to gather as much information as possible, fearing that he might overlook a critical detail.

The Consequence: Raj's meticulous approach led to missed trading opportunities. By the time he felt confident enough to execute a trade, the market had often moved, leaving him frustrated and fearing that he had lost out on potential profits.

The Redemption: Raj realized that his fear of making mistakes was causing him to miss out on profitable trades. He decided to implement a structured decision-making process. He set specific criteria for trade entry and exit and established a time limit for his research.

By embracing a more balanced approach, Raj was able to overcome his fear of making imperfect decisions and became more efficient in his trading. He understood that no amount of information could eliminate all risks, and he learned to trust his judgment while managing his fear of uncertainty effectively.

Trader Story 5: The Hasty Exit

Michael, an avid options trader, had a tendency to cash in on winning trades too quickly out of fear that the market might turn against him. His impulsive exits were hampering his risk-to-reward ratio in the long run.

The Fearful Reaction: Michael often felt an overwhelming fear of losing his hard-earned gains. Whenever a trade moved in his favor, he would hastily exit to secure profits, fearing that the market could reverse, eroding his gains and turning a winning trade into a losing one.

The Consequence: While Michael's strategy of locking in gains protected him from potential losses, it also meant that he was missing out on larger profits. His fear of relinquishing profits prematurely left him with a series of small wins but failed to maximize the potential of his trades.

The Redemption: Michael realized that his fear of losing was holding him back from achieving larger gains. He decided to adopt a more disciplined approach to his exits. He set specific profit-taking levels based on his analysis and trading plan and made a commitment to stick to them.

By maintaining discipline and not succumbing to fear-based exits, Michael found that his risk-to-reward ratio improved significantly. He understood that successful trading often required patience and the ability to let winning trades run their course. Over time, Michael's trading results reflected his newfound approach, with larger profits and a more balanced risk management strategy.

The key takeaway from these stories is that fear can be managed through education, discipline, risk management, and emotional awareness. By learning to control their fear, traders can make more rational decisions and ultimately achieve greater success in options trading. In the following chapters, we will delve into other common emotions and provide guidance on achieving emotional balance for optimal trading outcomes.

5. Cognitive Biases and Fallacies in Options Trading: Recognizing and Avoiding Pitfalls

Success isn't solely determined by market analysis and technical expertise. An often-underestimated aspect of trading is the profound influence of cognitive biases and fallacies on traders' decision-making processes. In this chapter, we will delve into the realms of biases, fallacies, and their interconnection. We will examine why traders are vulnerable to these cognitive pitfalls and how they impact options trading. Most importantly, we will explore strategies for recognizing and mitigating these biases and fallacies, empowering traders to make more rational and informed choices.

Understanding Biases and Fallacies:

In our decision-making process, we all have tendencies and errors that can lead us astray. These tendencies are what we call biases. They are like mental shortcuts that our brains take, often without us realizing it. Imagine trying to find your way through a maze; your brain sometimes takes the quickest path, even if it's not the best one.

Fallacies, on the other hand, are errors in our thinking. Think of them as traps or pitfalls in our reasoning. Fallacies are like the mirage of an oasis in the desert – they seem real at first glance, but they're actually illusions.

The Relationship Between Biases and Fallacies:

Biases often lead us into fallacies. They set the stage for us to make errors in our judgment or reasoning. It's like having fog on your car's windshield; it distorts your view, making it easier to drive into a pothole you didn't see.

For example, let's say you're buying a used car. You really like the color red, and you find a red car that you fall in love with. Your bias toward red cars influences you to focus only on the positive aspects of that particular car, ignoring any potential problems. This is a bias called the "preference bias." Your love for the color red (the bias) makes you ignore potential issues with the car (the fallacy).

In options trading, these biases and fallacies can lead to errors in judgment and potentially impact your trading decisions. It's essential to recognize these cognitive tendencies and the errors they can lead to so that you can make more informed and rational choices in the world of options trading.

Trading Mindtraps: Common Types of Biases and Fallacies

Confirmation Bias: Confirmation bias is the tendency to seek out, interpret, and remember information that confirms our preexisting beliefs or opinions while ignoring or dismissing information that contradicts them.

Example: Suppose an options trader is convinced that a particular stock will rise based on their initial analysis. They might only pay attention to positive news about the stock, ignore negative news, and discount any technical indicators suggesting a potential downturn. This bias can lead to overconfidence and risky trading decisions.

Overconfidence Bias: Overconfidence bias involves individuals overestimating their abilities or knowledge, often leading them to take excessive risks.

Example: An overconfident trader might believe they have an edge in predicting market movements and, as a result, take excessively large positions or neglect risk management strategies. This can result in significant losses if their confidence is unwarranted.

Anchoring Bias: Anchoring bias occurs when people rely too heavily on the first piece of information (the anchor) they encounter when making decisions.

Example: If a trader sees a stock's all-time high price and anchors to that price, they might be hesitant to sell the stock even when it has fallen significantly. This can lead to holding onto losing positions for too long.

Loss Aversion: Loss aversion is the tendency to prefer avoiding losses over acquiring equivalent gains, often leading to risk-averse behavior.

Example: A trader might hold onto a losing position for too long because they want to avoid realizing the loss, even when it's clear that the position is unlikely to recover. This can lead to missed opportunities to exit and cut losses.

Hindsight Bias: Hindsight bias is the belief that an event was predictable or foreseeable after it has already occurred.

Example: After a stock experiences a sharp drop, a trader might claim they knew it was going to happen all along, even if they didn't take any action to protect against the decline. This bias can lead to overconfidence in hindsight.

Availability Heuristic: This bias involves making decisions based on readily available information or recent experiences rather than conducting a comprehensive analysis.

Example: A trader might buy or sell options based on the latest news headline they saw without considering the broader market context. This can result in impulsive and poorly thought-out trades.

Recency Bias: Recency bias is the tendency to give more weight to recent events or information when making decisions.

Example: A trader might assume that a stock's recent strong performance will continue indefinitely, leading to a bias toward bullish positions. This bias can lead to overlooking longer-term trends and risks.

Sunk Cost Fallacy: Sunk cost fallacy is the inclination to continue investing in a decision or project based on the cumulative investments made, even when it's not rational to do so.

Example: A trader might hold onto a losing position because they've already invested a significant amount in it, rather than cutting losses as per their original plan. This can result in further losses.

Herding Behavior: Herding behavior involves following the actions of the majority or mimicking the behavior of others without conducting independent research.

Example: A trader might buy a particular option because they see many others doing the same, even if they don't fully understand the rationale behind the trade. This can lead to crowded trades and potential losses if the herd is wrong.

Framing Effect: The framing effect is the phenomenon where the way information is presented (or framed) can influence decision-making; individuals may react differently to the same information depending on how it is presented.

Example: In options trading, a trader might perceive a stock's price decline as a buying opportunity when framed positively as "correction," but as a risky move when framed negatively as "downturn."

Endowment Effect: The endowment effect is the tendency to overvalue items or assets simply because one owns them, making it difficult to sell or let go of those items even when it's financially sensible.

Example: A trader may hold onto options contracts because they own them, even when it's clear that selling them would be a more rational decision given the market conditions.

Self-Serving Bias: Self-serving bias is the inclination to attribute positive outcomes to one's own skills or actions but attribute negative outcomes to external factors or bad luck.

Example: When a trade goes well, a trader might credit their exceptional analysis skills, but when a trade goes poorly, they may blame market manipulation or unforeseen events.

Optimism Bias: Optimism bias is the belief that one is less likely to experience negative events and more likely to experience positive events than the average person.

Example: A trader may underestimate the risks associated with a particular strategy or underestimate the likelihood of a trade turning sour.

Dunning-Kruger Effect: The Dunning-Kruger effect is the cognitive bias wherein individuals with low competence or knowledge in a particular area tend to overestimate their ability in that area.

Example: An inexperienced trader might believe they have a deep understanding of options trading while lacking the necessary knowledge to make informed decisions.

Clustering Illusion: The clustering illusion is the tendency to perceive patterns or trends in random or unrelated data, often leading to incorrect conclusions.

Example: A trader may mistakenly believe that recent patterns in a stock's price movements indicate a predictable trend, even if the data is statistically random.

Gambler's Fallacy: The gambler's fallacy is the belief that past random events (like coin flips or dice rolls) can influence future outcomes, when in fact, each event is independent.

Example: A trader might believe that because a stock has declined for several days in a row, it's due for a price increase, ignoring the randomness of market movements.

Mere Exposure Effect: The mere exposure effect is the tendency to develop a preference for things merely because they are familiar or have been encountered repeatedly.

Example: A trader might favor a specific stock or asset class simply because they have been exposed to it frequently, even if there are more suitable alternatives.

Illusion of Control: The illusion of control is the belief that one has more control over events or outcomes than is realistic.

Example: A trader may think that they can control a stock's price movement by constantly monitoring it or using a specific trading strategy, despite the market's inherent unpredictability.

Groupthink: Groupthink is a bias that occurs within a group of people, where the desire for harmony or conformity in the group results in an irrational or dysfunctional decision-making outcome.

Example: A group of traders might collectively decide to follow a popular trading trend without critically evaluating the risks, leading to substantial losses for all involved.

Belief Perseverance: Belief perseverance is the tendency to cling to one's initial beliefs or opinions even in the face of contradictory evidence.

Example: A trader who strongly believes in a particular trading strategy may continue to use it despite consistent losses, ignoring evidence that suggests the strategy is not effective.

Authority Bias: Authority bias is the inclination to place undue trust in the opinions or recommendations of authority figures or experts.

Example: A trader may blindly follow the advice of a famous financial pundit without conducting their own analysis, leading to potentially poor investment decisions.

Fear of Missing Out (FOMO): Fear of missing out is the fear that others are profiting from opportunities, and one might miss out on those gains.

Example: FOMO can lead a trader to jump into a trade impulsively because they fear missing out on a sudden price surge, often without proper analysis or risk management.

Regret Aversion: Regret aversion is the desire to avoid making decisions that may lead to feelings of regret, even if those decisions have a higher expected value.

Example: A trader might avoid making a difficult decision to cut losses on a losing position because they fear regretting the decision if the stock rebounds.

Prospect Theory: Prospect theory is a cognitive bias related to how people make decisions involving risk and uncertainty, often emphasizing potential losses more than equivalent gains.

Example: A trader might be more averse to taking a position with a 10% chance of a significant loss, even if the expected value is positive, due to the fear of the potential loss.

Representativeness Heuristic: Representativeness heuristic is the tendency to judge the probability of an event based on how similar it is to a prototype or a stereotype.

Example: A trader might assume that a small, relatively unknown company's stock will perform poorly because it doesn't fit the prototype of a successful company, even if the fundamentals are strong.

Bandwagon Effect: The bandwagon effect is the tendency to adopt certain behaviors or beliefs because they are popular or widely accepted.

Example: A trader may buy a specific option because they see a growing number of other traders doing the same, without conducting their own analysis.

Money Illusion: Money illusion is the misperception of a change in the value of money, often due to not accounting for inflation or deflation.

Example: A trader may not adjust their trading strategies for changing economic conditions, assuming that nominal price changes are more significant than real (inflation-adjusted) changes.

Authority Misattribution: Authority misattribution is the tendency to ascribe expertise or authority to individuals or sources that may not be truly knowledgeable or reliable.

Example: A trader may assume that an online financial forum post is authoritative simply because it is well-written, without verifying the source's credibility.

Hyperbolic Discounting: Hyperbolic discounting is the preference for smaller, immediate rewards over larger, delayed rewards, even when the latter has higher overall value.

Example: A trader might opt for short-term, speculative options with the potential for quick gains over longer-term, safer investments with more significant potential returns.

Curse of Knowledge: The curse of knowledge is the difficulty of imagining or understanding what it's like not to know something that one is already knowledgeable about.

Example: An experienced options trader may struggle to communicate complex trading strategies to beginners, as they assume the knowledge level of the audience is the same as theirs.

Post-Purchase Rationalization: Post-purchase rationalization is the tendency to convince oneself that a purchase or decision was a good one after it has already been made.

Example: After buying an option that starts losing value, a trader may convince themselves that it was a wise decision and ignore signs indicating otherwise.

Outcome Bias: Outcome bias is the tendency to judge the quality of a decision based on its outcome rather than the quality of the decision-making process.

Example: If a trader takes a high-risk trade that happens to result in a profit, they may consider it a good decision, even if it was based on poor analysis and high risk.

Illusion of Validity: The illusion of validity is the belief that one's judgments and predictions are more accurate and valid than they truly are.

Example: A trader might believe their market predictions are always correct, even when there is no statistical evidence to support this belief.

Ostrich Effect: The ostrich effect is the tendency to avoid negative information or bury one's head in the sand, particularly when facing potential losses.

Example: A trader may ignore negative news about a stock they are heavily invested in, hoping that the issues will resolve themselves.

Why Traders Are Prone to Cognitive Biases and Fallacies:
Traders are susceptible to cognitive biases and fallacies due to a complex interplay of psychological, environmental, and experiential

factors. These elements can significantly influence how traders perceive information and make decisions in the options trading arena.

1. Psychological Factors:

Emotional Influences: Trading often triggers powerful emotions, including fear, greed, and excitement. These emotions can amplify cognitive biases. For instance, fear can enhance loss aversion bias, causing traders to hold onto losing positions due to the emotional pain of realizing losses.

Personality Traits: Individual personality traits also play a role. Some traders may possess a natural disposition toward certain biases, such as overconfidence or risk aversion, which can shape their decision-making processes.

2. Environmental Factors:

Cultural Influences: Cultural backgrounds and norms can significantly impact a trader's mindset and biases. Cultures that emphasize risk avoidance may encourage biases like loss aversion, where traders are averse to taking risks. Conversely, cultures that encourage entrepreneurial risk-taking may foster overconfidence.

Media and News: The media landscape plays a pivotal role in shaping traders' perceptions. Biased or sensationalized reporting can contribute to confirmation bias, as traders may be more inclined to rely on information that aligns with narratives presented in the media.

3. Experiential Factors:

Past Trading Experience: Previous successes and failures in trading can exert a lasting influence on biases. Traders who have experienced significant gains may develop overconfidence, while those who have faced substantial losses may become more risk-averse.

Educational Background: A trader's educational background can introduce biases stemming from specific disciplines. For example, individuals with a background in mathematics may be prone to anchoring fallacies, relying heavily on numerical data and statistical analysis.

4. Cultural Factors:

Communication Styles: Cultural differences in communication styles can impact how traders interpret and act on information. In cultures that emphasize group harmony, traders may exhibit herding behavior, following collective sentiment without conducting independent analysis. Moreover, confirmation bias can be influenced by cultural communication norms, leading traders to seek information that aligns with their cultural beliefs.

Managing Biases and Fallacies for Wise Decision Making
1. Recognize Cognitive Biases and Fallacies:

Education: The first step is awareness. Traders should educate themselves about common biases and fallacies that can affect decision-making in trading. Understand what these biases are, how they manifest, and the typical scenarios in which they occur.

Self-Reflection: Encourage traders to engage in regular self-reflection during and after trades. Ask questions like, "Am I making this decision based on data and analysis, or is it influenced by emotions or preconceived beliefs?" Self-awareness is the foundation of managing biases.

2. Emotional Discipline:

Emotion Management: Emotions often fuel biases and fallacies. Traders should develop emotional discipline through practices like mindfulness meditation or deep breathing exercises. These techniques help traders stay calm and rational in the face of market volatility.

Pre-trade Routine: Implement a pre-trade routine that includes a checklist to assess emotional readiness. This can help traders recognize when they are not in the right emotional state to make decisions and potentially delay trading until they are.

3. Objective Analysis:

Data-Driven Decisions: Emphasize the importance of data-driven decisions. Encourage traders to rely on objective analysis, such as technical and fundamental analysis, rather than intuition or gut feelings.

Alternative Perspectives: Challenge traders to actively seek out and consider alternative perspectives and information that contradicts their existing beliefs. This helps counteract confirmation bias and encourages a more balanced analysis.

4. Trading Plan:

Create and Stick to a Trading Plan: Developing a well-defined trading plan with clear entry and exit criteria helps remove impulsiveness and emotional reactions from decision-making. The plan should include risk management rules.

Review and Adjust: Regularly review and adjust the trading plan as needed to adapt to changing market conditions and personal growth as a trader.

5. Accountability and Feedback:

Trading Journal: Maintain a detailed trading journal that includes trade rationale, entry and exit points, emotions felt during the trade, and results. Regularly reviewing this journal provides insight into biases and areas for improvement.

Peer Review: Seek feedback from peers or mentors. Discussing trades with others can reveal biases that may not be apparent when analyzing trades alone.

6. Continuous Learning:

Stay Informed: Continue learning about trading strategies, market conditions, and psychology. Staying informed helps traders adapt to evolving market dynamics.

Regularly Assess Progress: Reflect on your trading journey and assess progress in managing biases. Celebrate successes and address areas that still need improvement.

7. Pause and Reflect:

Implement a Decision Pause: Before making a trading decision, take a moment to pause and reflect. This brief break can help traders reconsider their choices and assess whether biases are influencing them.

Biases and Fallacies: Trader Case Studies
Trader Story 1: The Unlucky Streak

Background: Robert had recently experienced a string of losing trades, influenced by the Gambler's Fallacy, which led him to believe that his luck was bound to change soon.

Influence: Robert made larger and riskier bets, assuming that his previous losses meant he was due for a winning streak, driven by the Gambler's Fallacy.

Consequences: His losses continued to mount as he misjudged market conditions and ignored sound trading strategies.

Resolution: Recognizing the Gambler's Fallacy in his thinking, Robert implemented a strict risk management plan. He began basing trades on market analysis rather than expecting luck to turn in his favor.

Trader Story 2: The Stubborn Investor

Background: Lisa purchased a call option for a particular stock at a higher price and saw the stock's value decline.

Influence: Lisa couldn't accept that the stock's value had dropped below her purchase price and refused to sell, a result of Anchoring Bias.

Consequences: The stock continued to plummet, causing substantial losses as Lisa remained anchored to her initial investment.

Resolution: After suffering significant losses, Lisa acknowledged the Anchoring Bias affecting her decision. She learned to set clear exit points based on market conditions and analysis rather than fixating on her original purchase price.

Trader Story 3: The Selective Information Trader

Background: David was bullish on a tech company and actively sought out positive news articles and reports about it.

Influence: David only considered information that confirmed his bullish view while ignoring negative indicators, succumbing to Confirmation Bias.

Consequences: The company faced unexpected challenges, resulting in a sharp decline in its stock price, and David incurred substantial losses.

Resolution: Recognizing the Confirmation Bias at play, David actively sought diverse perspectives and information that challenged his beliefs. This allowed for a more balanced approach to decision-making.

Trader Story 4: The Guru Follower

Background: Michael admired a well-known financial expert and followed their trading recommendations without question, influenced by Authority Bias.

Influence: Michael gave undue weight to the authority's recommendations, blindly executing trades without conducting his own analysis, driven by Authority Bias.

Consequences: Some of the recommended trades turned out to be poorly timed, resulting in losses that Michael hadn't anticipated.

Resolution: Acknowledging his tendency to succumb to Authority Bias, Michael started to validate expert recommendations with his own analysis. He gradually developed more independent trading skills and reduced his reliance on external authority figures.

Trader Story 5: The Alluring Outcome Bias

Background: Sarah had been successful in her previous options trades, leading her to overestimate her abilities and develop an Outcome Bias.

Influence: Sarah believed that because her past trades had resulted in profits, her current trades were sure to succeed, even without thorough analysis.

Consequences: Ignoring critical market signals, Sarah experienced substantial losses when her assumptions proved incorrect.

Resolution: Sarah recognized the Outcome Bias influencing her decisions and began conducting more rigorous analysis for each trade, focusing on potential risks rather than being solely swayed by past outcomes.

Trader Story 6: The Bandwagon Effect

Background: John noticed that many traders in his network were jumping on the same trade, creating a Bandwagon Effect.

Influence: John felt compelled to join the trade simply because others were doing it, without conducting independent research.

Consequences: The overcrowded trade resulted in heightened volatility, and John suffered losses as the market sentiment suddenly shifted.

Resolution: Learning from this experience, John decided to conduct his own analysis and make decisions based on his own research rather than following the crowd blindly.

Trader Story 7: Fear of Missing Out (FOMO)

Background: Emily observed that a particular stock had been surging in value, leading to a strong Fear of Missing Out (FOMO).

Influence: Fearful of missing out on potential gains, Emily hastily entered the trade without conducting proper analysis.

Consequences: The stock's value quickly plummeted, causing Emily to incur significant losses as her impulsive decision backfired.

Resolution: Emily realized the impact of FOMO on her trading and committed to a more disciplined approach. She vowed to carefully analyze opportunities before jumping into trades.

Trader Story 8: The Dunning-Kruger Effect

Background: Mark, a novice trader, believed he was an expert after a few successful trades, displaying the Dunning-Kruger Effect.

Influence: Overconfident in his abilities, Mark traded aggressively and ignored advice from more experienced traders.

Consequences: Mark's overconfidence led to a series of poor decisions, resulting in substantial losses and a humbling experience.

Resolution: Mark recognized the Dunning-Kruger Effect had led him astray. He sought mentorship from experienced traders and focused on continuous learning.

Trader Story 9: The Self-Serving Bias

Background: Alex had a tendency to attribute his successes to his skills while blaming external factors for losses, demonstrating the Self-Serving Bias.

Influence: Alex failed to critically evaluate his trading decisions, always assuming he was right.

Consequences: This bias prevented Alex from learning from his mistakes and adapting his trading strategies, he repeated his mistakes making substantial losses.

Resolution: Acknowledging the Self-Serving Bias, Alex began taking responsibility for both wins and losses, using each experience as an opportunity for improvement.

Trader Story 10: The Influential Framing Effect

Background: Jenny received a stock tip presented in a highly positive light by a financial news outlet, succumbing to the Framing Effect.

Influence: She invested heavily in the stock without considering potential downsides due to the overly positive framing.

Consequences: The stock's value dropped significantly, leading Jenny to substantial losses because she hadn't considered the negative aspects.

Resolution: Jenny realized the impact of framing on her decisions and decided to critically evaluate information sources and consider different perspectives before making trading choices.

In closing, the exploration of cognitive biases and fallacies in the context of options trading psychology reveals the profound impact these psychological tendencies can have on traders' decisions and outcomes. These biases and fallacies, whether driven by overconfidence, social pressures, or skewed perceptions of reality, can lead traders down a perilous path of poor judgment and costly mistakes.

However, the stories we've encountered in this chapter also illustrate a crucial point: awareness and recognition of these biases and fallacies are the first steps toward mitigating their influence. Just as the traders in our narratives learned from their experiences, acknowledging these cognitive pitfalls empowers us to become more mindful, rational, and disciplined traders.

As you venture further into the world of options trading, remember that no trader is entirely immune to cognitive biases and fallacies. They are ingrained in human psychology. Yet, by diligently applying the strategies and exercises discussed in this chapter, you can strive to minimize their impact on your decision-making.

6. Hope: Balancing Optimism and Realism in Options Trading

Hope takes on a dual role, akin to a luminous beacon guiding traders toward success or a treacherous abyss that can swallow them whole. This section delves deep into the multifaceted nature of hope within the context of options trading, exploring its profound influence on trading decisions and providing vivid examples to illustrate its impact.

The Nature of Hope in Options Trading:

Hope in options trading is a psychological phenomenon that can be both a trader's greatest ally and their worst enemy. At its core, it is the unwavering belief that one's trades will result in favorable outcomes, accompanied by the expectation of a prosperous financial future. This sentiment often provides traders with the motivation and courage to navigate the complexities of the options market. However, it also carries the potential to lead traders astray when hope morphs into irrational optimism.

Example: Consider a trader who enters a bullish options position on a tech stock, fervently hoping for a substantial price surge. This hope stems from the belief that the stock will rally, anticipating a profitable trade.

Impact of Hope on Trading Decisions:

Hope can exert a profound influence on the decision-making process of options traders. When it is harnessed judiciously, it can serve as a source of inspiration, encouraging calculated risk-taking and innovation. Conversely, when unchecked, it can lead to a host of cognitive biases and detrimental behaviors that may result in significant financial losses.

Example: Imagine a scenario in which a trader, spurred by hope, disregards a predetermined stop-loss order in the anticipation of a miraculous reversal. This behavior is rooted in the belief that the trade will ultimately turn profitable, despite mounting evidence to the contrary

Triggers of Hope: What Ignites the Flame?
Optimistic Market Sentiment:

Positive News Flow: News of a breakthrough in technology, a successful clinical trial, or favorable economic indicators can trigger hope. Traders may become excessively optimistic when surrounded by a stream of positive news.

Example: A trader, influenced by news of a new product launch, invests in call options on a tech company, anticipating a surge in stock price.

Bullish Market Trends: During periods of sustained market rallies, hope can flourish. Bullish trends often lead traders to expect ongoing gains, sometimes overlooking potential reversals.

Example: A trader becomes increasingly optimistic as they witness a prolonged bull market, prompting them to open multiple bullish options positions.

Pessimistic Market Sentiment:

Market Downturns: Conversely, periods of market downturns can trigger hope, albeit of a pessimistic nature. Traders may hope for a market rebound when faced with losses, sometimes leading to hasty decisions.

Example: A trader, experiencing losses during a bear market, clings to the hope that the market will soon recover, delaying strategic exits.

Fear of Missing Out (FOMO): The fear of missing out on potential profits can drive traders to enter positions hastily. They hope that they can catch up with a rapidly rising market.

Example: A trader, fearing they missed a significant price jump, impulsively buys call options without conducting thorough analysis.

Past Experiences:

Recency Bias: Recent experiences, particularly those where losing trades turned positive after hitting stop-loss levels, can trigger hope. Traders may believe that history will repeat itself.

Example: A trader recalls an instance where a trade reversed and became profitable after hitting a stop-loss, leading them to hope for a similar outcome in a new trade.

Past Successes: Past profitable trades often leave an indelible mark on a trader's psyche, leading them to hope for a repeat performance. This can sometimes result in overconfidence.

Example: A trader who enjoyed substantial gains from a specific options strategy may feel overly confident in its effectiveness, even in different market conditions.

Market Speculation:

Speculative Opportunities: Traders may encounter speculative opportunities where the potential for massive gains fuels hope. They may hope for an improbable, lucrative outcome.

Example: A trader invests in far out-of-the-money call options on a volatile cryptocurrency, hoping for an extraordinary price surge.

Market Rumors: Rumors and unverified information can kindle hope, prompting traders to act on hearsay rather than concrete data.

Example: A trader acts on a market rumor of an impending merger, hoping to profit from the speculated price increase.

Irrational Exuberance: Periods of exuberance in the market, where euphoria runs high, can trigger unrealistic hope. Traders may hope for limitless gains without considering potential downsides.

Example: A trader, caught up in the euphoria of a speculative bubble, hopes that a rapidly rising asset will continue its ascent indefinitely.

Understanding these triggers of hope in options trading is crucial for traders to maintain emotional balance. It allows them to recognize when hope is driving their decisions and take measured steps to ensure their trading strategies remain grounded in reality. By acknowledging both optimistic and pessimistic triggers, traders can make informed decisions that align with their goals and risk tolerance while avoiding impulsive actions driven solely by hope.

Managing Hope: The Art of Balanced Expectations

In the tumultuous terrain of options trading, hope stands as the most perilous emotion, surpassing even fear, greed, or regret in its potential to wreak havoc. Imagine a scenario where a losing trade, clung to tenaciously due to the intoxicating allure of hope, swiftly transforms a thriving trading account into a barren wasteland. It's a stark reality that underscores the paramount importance of mastering hope's influence. To navigate the intricate web of options trading successfully, one must become adept at managing hope. In the upcoming techniques, we will explore a set of techniques and strategies to achieve precisely that, transforming hope from a reckless adversary into a steady ally on the journey toward trading proficiency and financial stability.

1. Construct a "Hope Diary":

Create a journal dedicated solely to tracking your emotional responses to trades. Record moments when hope sways your decisions and categorize them into optimistic or pessimistic instances. Write down your thought processes and the outcomes.

This exercise helps you recognize patterns and tendencies in your trading behavior.

Example: You notice that after a series of profitable trades, you tend to become overly optimistic and increase your position sizes. Later, when some of these trades turn negative, you suffer substantial losses. By keeping a hope diary, you become aware of this pattern and can take corrective action.

2. Utilize a "Reality Checklist":

Develop a checklist that you refer to before making any trading decisions. List both the optimistic and pessimistic factors influencing your trade. By objectively assessing these factors, you can balance your hope with a realistic perspective. This tool acts as a counterbalance to emotional biases.

Example: Before entering a trade, you review your reality checklist. While optimistic factors may include a strong earnings report, you also consider pessimistic factors like potential market volatility. This exercise keeps your expectations grounded.

3. The "Two-Strike Rule":

Implement a rule that requires two pieces of evidence supporting a trade before committing. If one factor is purely hopeful or speculative, it doesn't qualify. This approach forces you to rely on a more comprehensive analysis, reducing impulsive decisions driven by unfounded optimism.

Example: You come across a stock tip on a social media forum, which triggers your hope for quick profits. However, you require a second piece of evidence, such as a technical indicator aligning with the tip, to validate the trade.

4. Practice "Mindful Trading":

Incorporate mindfulness techniques into your trading routine. Before executing a trade, take a few minutes to focus on your breath, clear your mind of expectations, and observe your thoughts and emotions. This practice helps you detach from the emotional rollercoaster of hope and make more rational decisions.

Example: Before entering a trade, you engage in a brief mindfulness exercise, acknowledging any hopeful feelings without letting them cloud your judgment.

5. Engage in "Scenario Planning":

Anticipate various scenarios for each trade, including worst-case outcomes. By mentally preparing for losses and setbacks, you reduce the emotional impact of unmet expectations. This exercise also helps you develop contingency plans.

Example: Before entering an options trade, you imagine scenarios where the trade goes south. You consider how you would react, whether you'd cut losses, and what alternative strategies you could employ.

6. "Peer Feedback Circle":

Establish a group of trusted trader peers or mentors who can provide honest feedback on your trades and emotional responses. Sharing your experiences and receiving input from others can provide valuable perspectives and help you manage hope more effectively.

Example: You regularly discuss your trades and emotional challenges with a group of experienced traders. They offer insights and strategies based on their own experiences, helping you gain a more balanced perspective.

7. Embrace "Outcome Detachment":

Shift your focus away from immediate trade outcomes and concentrate on the process and discipline of trading. Recognize that individual trades are part of a larger portfolio and that success is measured over the long term, not by a single trade.

Example: Instead of obsessing over whether a specific options trade will be profitable, you concentrate on adhering to your trading plan and maintaining discipline, regardless of the outcome.

By incorporating these creative techniques and exercises into your trading routine, you can effectively manage the powerful emotion of hope. These strategies promote a balanced perspective, ensuring that hope becomes a constructive force that inspires disciplined, rational decisions rather than an impulsive driver of unrealistic expectations. Mastering the art of balanced expectations is essential for long-term success in the world of options trading

Hope: Trader Case Studies
Trader Story 1: The Costly Cling to Hope

Meet Sarah, a seasoned options trader with a penchant for optimism. Sarah had always prided herself on her ability to see the silver lining in any trade. However, her unwavering hope was about to put her to the ultimate test.

The Hopeful Gamble: One fateful morning, Sarah entered into a complex options trade, convinced that it was destined for greatness. As the trade initially took a downward turn, her hope in a miraculous reversal held steadfast. She believed that market forces would eventually align in her favor.

The Consequence: Days turned into weeks, and Sarah's losing trade refused to budge. Yet, driven by her unshakable hope, she clung to the position, refusing to cut her losses. In her mind, the trade simply had to turn around; after all, she had seen such turnarounds before.

The Catastrophe: Unfortunately, the market had different plans. The trade spiraled further into the red, eventually culminating in a catastrophic loss that wiped out a significant portion of her trading account. Sarah's once-healthy balance now teetered on the brink of disaster.

The Awakening: Sarah's financial setback was not just a hit to her account; it was a wake-up call. She realized that her unbridled hope, while a source of motivation, had also led to a perilous lack of discipline. She had allowed hope to cloud her judgment and to justify holding onto losing positions far longer than she should have.

Determined to reclaim her trading prowess, Sarah embarked on a journey of self-discovery and strategy refinement. She sought mentorship from experienced traders who emphasized the importance of setting clear exit strategies and adhering to them. Sarah learned to balance her hope with a more structured approach, ensuring that her trades were grounded in realistic expectations.

In time, Sarah regained her footing in the options market. Her newfound ability to manage hope effectively allowed her to make rational decisions and avoid the perils of holding onto losing positions indefinitely. Sarah's story serves as a poignant reminder that while hope can be a guiding light, it must be tempered with discipline to ensure long-term success in the world of options trading.

Trader Story 2: The Gambler's Fallacy

Meet Alex, a trader whose journey would be marked by a fateful encounter with hope, the gambler's fallacy, and the painful lessons learned in the world of options trading.

The Initial Misstep: One sunny morning, Alex took a position in a promising stock, believing it was poised for substantial gains. However, as the day unfolded, the stock began to steadily decline, triggering Alex's mental stop-loss level.

The Hopeful Hesitation: Despite his trading plan and the prudent decision to cut his losses, hope seized Alex's rationality. He clung to the trade, hoping for a miraculous turnaround. He convinced himself that the stock simply had to rebound, citing past instances where similar situations had ended favorably.

The Gambler's Fallacy: Days turned into weeks, and the stock's downward trajectory showed no signs of abating. Rather than adhering to his stop-loss strategy, Alex succumbed to the gambler's fallacy. He convinced himself that the stock's relentless descent was statistically improbable and that a reversal was imminent.

The Dangerous Escalation: Fueled by this irrational belief, Alex took increasingly desperate measures. He poured more capital into the losing trade, convinced that a few points in his favor would not only break even but also yield substantial profits. He even sold other assets to bolster his position in the ill-fated stock.

The Total Wipeout: Regrettably, the market continued to defy Alex's unwavering hope. The stock plunged further, eroding his account balance steadily. In a cruel twist of fate, his entire trading account was wiped out entirely, leaving him with nothing but regret and a harsh lesson learned.

The Redemption: Alex's path to recovery was a long and arduous one. He spent years meticulously saving and honing his trading discipline. He vowed never to let hope cloud his judgment again and to always respect his predefined stop-loss levels.

In time, Alex returned to the world of options trading with newfound wisdom and a disciplined mindset. His painful encounter with hope and the gambler's fallacy had transformed him into a more prudent trader. His story serves as a poignant reminder that managing hope is not just about mitigating losses; it's about safeguarding one's trading journey and financial future from the pitfalls of irrational optimism.

Trader Story 3: The Desperate Gamble

Meet James, a trader whose journey would be marked by a fateful encounter with hope, reckless optimism, and the steep price paid in the world of options trading.

The Fateful Day: It was the expiry day of options, an occasion known for its volatility and high-risk potential. James, fueled by an insatiable desire for quick riches, decided to dive into the fray. He took multiple low-probability trades, hoping to hit the jackpot and become a millionaire in a single day.

The Erosion of Hope: As the trading day progressed, James' options slowly eroded in value, even though the market moved partially in his favor. Despite witnessing his trades losing ground, hope kept him on the edge. He convinced himself that the market would make a miraculous swing, turning his losing positions into a fortune.

The Dangerous Averaging: Slowly but surely, James started pouring additional funds into his deteriorating trades, averaging down his position sizes. He believed that with enough capital added to the trades, a slight movement in his favor would bring him back to profitability. He poured everything he could into these high-stakes gambles.

The Desperate Plea: As the clock ticked closer to expiration, James's desperation reached a fever pitch. He locked himself in his bedroom, beseeching and praying to a higher power. He knelt, he bowed, and he begged for a miraculous market reversal that would save him from financial ruin. It was a ritual he had performed multiple times in the past, often escaping unscathed.

The Costly Lesson: Unfortunately, this time was different. The options expired worthless, and James was left with a substantial loss that wiped out his trading capital entirely. It was a bitter pill to swallow, but it was a lesson he could no longer ignore.

The Redemption: James made the difficult decision to step away from trading for five long years. During this hiatus, he diligently saved and, more importantly, reflected on his past mistakes. He realized that hope, combined with reckless gambling, had nearly cost him everything.

Upon his return to the world of options trading, James had transformed into a disciplined, prudent trader. He vowed never to let hope blind him again. His story serves as a stark reminder of the dangers of trading on mere hope and the importance of disciplined risk management in the pursuit of long-term success.

Trader Story 4: Escaping the Snare of Outcome Bias

Meet Rachel, a trader whose journey would be defined by her encounter with hope, the pitfalls of a faulty strategy, and the crucial realization that would reshape her approach to options trading.

The Bold Gambit: On a particularly eventful trading day, Rachel found herself in the midst of a high-risk endeavor. She had taken multiple out-of-the-money options trades, each with a low probability of success, all on the brink of expiration. Her audacious plan was to break even, at best, but hope whispered that fortune might favor the bold.

The Slow Erosion: As the hours ticked away, Rachel's options started to erode in value. Yet, against the backdrop of a market partially moving in her favor, hope refused to relinquish its hold. She was determined to escape with at least a break-even outcome, believing that a miraculous market shift could be right around the corner.

The Tumultuous Ride: Instead of doubling down on her losses, Rachel maintained her original positions, waiting for the market to turn in her favor. As the final moments before expiration approached, the market did indeed make a favorable move, just enough to bring her trades back to breakeven.

The Realization: Rachel had technically escaped the abyss, and her trading account remained intact. However, she couldn't ignore the nagging feeling that her strategy had been fundamentally flawed. She understood that her escape from loss was more a result of luck and market randomness than a sound trading plan.

The Turning Point: Rather than succumbing to the dangerous allure of outcome bias, Rachel took a step back and critically assessed her approach. She realized that her strategy had relied too heavily on hope and lacked a clear, rational foundation. Recognizing the need for change, she set out to refine her trading tactics immediately.

The Redemption: Rachel reconfigured her approach to options trading. She sought to balance optimism with a sound strategy grounded in analysis and risk management. She was determined to ensure that her success was not merely the result of a fortunate outcome but rather the product of a disciplined and sustainable approach.

In the end, Rachel's story serves as a powerful reminder of the importance of recognizing the influence of hope and outcome bias in trading. Her willingness to adapt and evolve as a trader underscores the resilience required to thrive in the unpredictable world of options trading.

7: From Regret to Growth: Thriving in Options Trading

The Nature of Regret in Options Trading:

Regret is an ever-present companion, an emotion that carries lessons and insights waiting to be unearthed. This chapter delves into the intricate terrain of regret, dissecting its various forms, exploring the triggers that lead traders down this emotional path, and shedding light on how it impacts decision-making and trading outcomes. Yet, it's not merely an exploration of the shadows but a journey toward finding the silver lining within regret—a path to growth and resilience.

Why traders feel this emotion?

Missed Opportunities: This form of regret frequently looms over traders when they reflect on the opportunities they let slip through their fingers. It's the "what could have been" scenario, where traders ponder the wealth they might have accrued had they seized a particular trade or acted differently. Missed opportunities regret serves as a poignant reminder of the importance of recognizing and capitalizing on favorable market moments.

Decision Remorse: Regret can also emerge from specific trading decisions. Traders may find themselves haunted by impulsive actions or choices that deviated from their carefully crafted trading plans. Decision remorse often accompanies financial losses and acts as a demanding teacher, emphasizing the critical role of disciplined and well-informed decision-making in options trading. Below are some examples

1. Trading Against the Trend

Trading against the prevailing market trend is a common source of regret for options traders. This decision often arises from a belief that the market will reverse, but it can result in losses when the trend persists. Traders may regret not aligning their positions with the dominant market direction, especially when they fail to recognize the strength and sustainability of the trend.

2. Overtrading

Overtrading, or excessively frequent trading, often leads to regret. Traders may take on too many positions simultaneously or engage in high-frequency trading, which can lead to increased transaction costs and emotional exhaustion. Regret sets in when overtrading results in financial losses or missed opportunities due to an inability to manage numerous positions effectively.

3. Trading Based on Tips or Rumors

Relying on hot tips or market rumors without conducting thorough research can be a recipe for regret in options trading. Traders who follow such tips may find themselves in positions that don't align with their trading strategies or risk tolerance. Regret emerges when these tips or rumors fail to materialize as expected, potentially resulting in losses.

4. Ignoring Fundamental or Technical Analysis

Failure to utilize fundamental or technical analysis when making trading decisions can lead to decision remorse. Traders who disregard these analytical tools may lack a comprehensive understanding of the underlying factors driving the market. This can result in regret when trades turn unfavorable due to a lack of informed decision-making.

5. Chasing Performance

Chasing performance occurs when traders enter trades based on recent exceptional gains in the hope of replicating those results. However, markets are dynamic, and past performance doesn't guarantee future success. Traders may regret chasing performance when trades don't yield the expected results, leading to losses.

6. Emotional Decision-Making

Emotional decision-making, such as trading out of fear or greed, often leads to regrets. Emotional traders may make impulsive decisions that deviate from their rational trading plans. Regret sets in when these emotionally driven actions result in losses or missed opportunities.

Outcome Evaluation Regret: This form of regret arises when traders judge their past decisions solely based on their outcomes, rather than assessing the quality of their decision-making process. It leads to regret when a profitable trade turns into a loss or when a losing trade miraculously becomes profitable. Outcome evaluation regret highlights the importance of focusing on the decision-making process rather than being overly influenced by results.

The Impact of Regret on Options Trading:

Regret is not a passive emotion; it wields significant influence over a trader's behavior and performance in the options market. In this section, we'll delve into the profound impact of regret on options trading, shedding light on how it can affect traders' decisions and overall trading outcomes.

1. Revenge Trading: A Vicious Cycle

One of the most insidious effects of regret in options trading is the phenomenon known as "revenge trading." This occurs when a trader, consumed by the desire to recover losses incurred due to regrettable decisions, engages in impulsive and high-risk trading actions. Revenge trading often leads to a vicious cycle of further losses, exacerbating the initial regret and emotional turmoil.

Example: Sarah, a seasoned options trader, experienced a significant loss after ignoring her trading plan during a volatile market period. Fueled by regret and a determination to recoup her losses, she immediately entered a series of high-risk trades in an attempt to reverse her fortune. However, these impulsive actions only resulted in additional losses, further deepening her regret and emotional distress.

2. Reduced Confidence: The Silent Consequence

Regret can erode a trader's confidence, leaving them hesitant to execute well-researched trades. Traders who've experienced regret may become overly cautious, fearing that any decision, even those supported by strong analysis, will lead to further disappointment. This reduced confidence can hinder traders from seizing profitable opportunities and adhering to their trading plans.

3. Emotional Turmoil: Affecting Decision-Making

Regret often generates emotional turmoil, clouding a trader's judgment and leading to impulsive actions. Emotional decision-making can derail even the most well-thought-out trading plans, causing traders to deviate from their strategies and potentially incur further losses. Emotional turmoil can also lead to stress and anxiety, making it difficult for traders to remain focused and disciplined in their trading activities.

4. Paralysis by Analysis: Overthinking and Second-Guessing

Regret can lead to a state of overthinking and second-guessing. Traders who have experienced regret may find themselves constantly questioning their decisions and hesitating to enter or exit trades. This over-analysis can result in missed opportunities and a lack of confidence in one's trading strategy.

5. Suboptimal Risk Management

Regret can also impact a trader's approach to risk management. Traders who have experienced losses due to regret may become overly conservative in their risk management practices, setting excessively tight stop-loss orders or avoiding trades altogether. While risk management is essential, an excessive focus on avoiding regret can hinder a trader's ability to take calculated risks and achieve their trading goals.

6. Impact on Long-Term Goals

Regret can have a long-lasting impact on a trader's confidence and commitment to their long-term trading goals. Traders who have experienced significant regret may question their ability to succeed in the market and may even consider abandoning their trading journey altogether.

Recognizing these multifaceted consequences of regret is crucial for options traders. It highlights the need for effective strategies to manage and navigate this emotion, ensuring that it doesn't hinder a trader's ability to make rational decisions and achieve their trading objectives. In the upcoming sections, we will explore strategies for mitigating the negative impact of regret and harnessing its transformative potential.

Avenues to steer clear of regret's pitfalls
1. Predefined Decision Rules:

Establish strict rules for entry and exit points for each trade in your trading plan.

Adhere to these rules regardless of market conditions or emotional impulses, reducing room for regrettable decisions.

2. Regret Analysis:

Conduct a structured post-trade analysis for each position, whether it's a winning or losing trade.

Assess what went well and what could have been done differently to minimize future regrets.

3. Regret Minimization Framework:

Before entering a trade, ask yourself, "What could I regret about this trade?"

Identify potential sources of regret and take precautions to address them in your trading plan.

4. Collaborative Decision-Making:

Consider discussing your trading decisions with a trusted friend, mentor, or trading partner.

External perspectives can help you avoid impulsive choices and minimize regret.

5. Gradual Position Building:

Instead of taking a large position all at once, consider scaling into a trade over multiple smaller transactions.

This approach allows you to assess market conditions more gradually and reduces the chances of immediate regret.

6. Risk Assessment Framework:

Develop a comprehensive risk assessment framework that considers both financial and emotional risks.

Factor in how a potential trade might affect your overall financial well-being and emotional state.

7. Regret-Resistant Strategies:

Explore trading strategies that inherently reduce the potential for regret.

For example, some traders prefer defined-risk strategies like credit spreads to limit downside exposure.

8. Regret Scenario Planning:

Anticipate potential scenarios and their associated regrets.

Develop contingency plans for different outcomes to reduce the emotional impact of unexpected events.

9. Post-Trade Decompression:

After closing a trade, take a moment to decompress before making your next move.

This pause allows you to process any emotional reactions and make more rational decisions.

10. Continuous Education:

- Invest in ongoing education to stay informed about market dynamics and trading strategies. A well-informed trader is better equipped to make confident decisions and minimize regret.

11. Exit Strategies:

- Incorporate various exit strategies into your trading plan, such as trailing stops or target profit levels. Having predefined exit points reduces the likelihood of holding onto losing positions out of hope.

12. Trade Simulation:

- Use paper trading or trade simulation platforms to practice your strategies without real capital at risk. Simulated trades allow you to gain experience and build confidence before trading with real money.

By integrating these specific strategies into your options trading approach, you can proactively manage and reduce the emotion of regret. These methods focus on building resilience and emotional intelligence, allowing you to make more rational and disciplined decisions in the ever-changing world of options trading.

Regret: Trader Case Studies
Trader Story 1: The Lost Opportunity

Meet Sarah, an experienced options trader known for her cautious approach to the market. One day, she was meticulously researching potential trades and came across a stock with compelling options. Her analysis suggested that it had strong growth potential, but she hesitated, as she had recently suffered a small loss on a similar trade.

The Regrettable Hesitation: Sarah's hesitation stemmed from her recent setback, which had caused her to question her judgment. She decided to pass on the opportunity, fearing that history might repeat itself. The stock indeed surged in the following days, confirming her initial analysis.

The Consequence: As Sarah watched the stock climb, a profound sense of regret settled in. She realized that her hesitation had cost her a significant profit. She had missed a golden opportunity due to her fear of repeating past mistakes. The regret was palpable, leaving her feeling frustrated and disappointed.

The Redemption: Recognizing that regret was a natural part of trading, Sarah decided to learn from her experience. She revised her trading plan to include guidelines for managing hesitation and regret. She vowed not to let past setbacks paralyze her in the face of future opportunities.

Sarah started incorporating a structured decision-making process into her trading routine. Before passing on any opportunity, she thoroughly assessed the risk and reward, factored in her past experiences, and sought advice from her trading network.

Over time, Sarah became more adept at managing her regrets. She used them as stepping stones toward more informed decisions and greater self-awareness. Her newfound resilience allowed her to seize future opportunities with confidence, and she gradually made up for the missed profit by applying her refined approach.

Sarah's story serves as a reminder that regret can be a powerful motivator for growth and improvement in the world of options trading. By acknowledging and learning from her past hesitations, she transformed regret into a valuable resource for her trading journey.

Trader Story 2: The Vengeance Trade

Meet Alex, an options trader with a track record of careful decision-making and disciplined trading. One day, after a string of consecutive losses, he felt a growing sense of frustration and anger. He was determined to recover his losses, even if it meant deviating from his well-thought-out trading plan.

The Vengeance Trade: Fueled by emotions, Alex took a risky position in a highly volatile stock, doubling his usual position size. He was convinced that he could quickly recoup his losses and then some. However, the market had different plans, and his trade went against him.

The Consequence: As days turned into weeks, Alex watched in despair as the trade spiraled further into the red. What was initially an attempt to recover losses had now become a grave threat to his trading capital. His account was down by a staggering 50%, and the weight of regret was unbearable.

The Redemption: Alex eventually recognized the destructive nature of his revenge trading. He decided to take a step back and reflect on his actions. With a clear mind, he assessed the damage and realized that he needed to change his approach.

Alex accepted that recouping a 50% loss required making a 100% profit, a challenging feat. He understood that revenge trading had only dug him deeper into a hole. Instead, he adopted a patient and disciplined strategy.

Over time, Alex rebuilt his trading capital through careful risk management and strategic trading decisions. He focused on preserving his capital and steadily growing it, rather than chasing quick profits. He made a conscious effort to control his emotions and not let anger or regret drive his trading decisions.

Through persistence and a commitment to learning from his mistakes, Alex gradually recovered his losses and, more importantly, gained a deeper understanding of the importance of emotional control in trading. His story serves as a powerful reminder of the dangers of revenge trading and the potential for redemption through discipline and self-reflection in the world of options trading.

Trader Story 3: The Lesson of Sustainable Trading

Meet Daniel, an options trader who had recently experienced a windfall profit from a high-risk, speculative trade. Initially, he celebrated his success and the substantial gains he had made. However, as the days passed, he began to feel a sense of unease and regret.

The Regrettable Gain: Daniel had placed a bold bet on a highly volatile stock, and against the odds, it had paid off handsomely. His account had swelled with profits, but the euphoria soon gave way to a nagging feeling of unease. He realized that the trade's success was more due to luck than skill, and he couldn't replicate such gains consistently.

The Consequence: Rather than bask in the glory of his fleeting success, Daniel took a step back to assess the situation. He recognized that the strategy he had used was unsustainable and carried an extremely high risk of wiping out his account. The regret he felt was not about losing money but about the realization that he had been gambling rather than trading.

The Redemption: Determined to rectify his approach, Daniel made a crucial decision. He immediately shifted his trading strategy to prioritize consistency and risk management over short-term gains. He started by cutting his position size significantly to reduce risk exposure.

Daniel also focused on learning more about risk-adjusted strategies and options trading fundamentals. He sought out educational resources, joined trading communities, and consulted with experienced traders to gain a deeper understanding of sustainable trading practices.

Over time, Daniel's trading results became more stable and consistent. While he was no longer experiencing the roller-coaster of extreme gains and losses, he was steadily growing his account in a sustainable manner. He felt a sense of accomplishment and fulfillment, knowing that he was trading responsibly and adhering to sound principles.

Daniel's story serves as a valuable lesson in recognizing the dangers of outcome bias and the importance of trading with a sustainable, long-term perspective. By acknowledging his regret and taking immediate corrective action, he transformed his trading approach and achieved consistent success in the world of options trading.

8: Trading Discipline: Building the Mental Fortitude of a Successful Trader

In the ever-shifting landscape of options trading, where uncertainty reigns supreme and emotional turbulence can wreak havoc on a trader's journey, one attribute stands as a beacon of resilience and stability: discipline. The art of trading discipline is a cornerstone of success, a mental fortitude that separates the enduring trader from the impulsive gambler. In this chapter, we embark on a profound exploration of trading discipline, delving deep into its essence, its undeniable significance, and the practical strategies for its cultivation.

Understanding Trading Discipline

Trading discipline is the unwavering commitment to adhering to a well-defined trading plan, a set of rules and principles that guide every action in the market. It encompasses the ability to maintain composure in the face of both triumph and adversity, making decisions based on reason rather than emotion. A disciplined trader resists the siren call of impulsivity, avoids reckless risks, and stays the course even when the winds of uncertainty howl.

Trading discipline extends beyond the execution of trades. It is a comprehensive mindset that governs every facet of a trader's journey, from risk management and position sizing to entry and exit strategies. It is the keystone upon which consistent profitability and longevity in the market are built.

The Crucial Role of Discipline in Options Trading

In the complex realm of options trading, where volatility and unpredictability are constant companions, discipline serves as the compass guiding traders through turbulent waters. It is the guardian of capital preservation, the sentinel against impulsive decisions that can lead to devastating losses.

Without discipline, the allure of quick riches can entice traders into dangerous gambles, where a single reckless move can unravel months of hard-earned gains. Discipline provides the restraint needed to avoid overtrading, chasing losses, or falling prey to the temptation of high-risk strategies.

Cultivating Trading Discipline

Building trading discipline is not an overnight endeavor; it is a journey of self-mastery and continuous improvement. Below are key strategies and insights to help traders cultivate this indispensable trait:

1. Clear Trading Plan:

A well-defined trading plan with precise entry and exit rules serves as the bedrock of discipline.

Example: Sarah's trading plan includes specific criteria for entering a trade, the maximum risk she's willing to take, and predetermined profit targets. This plan keeps her focused on her strategy and minimizes impulsive decisions.

2. Risk Management:

Discipline begins with risk management. Traders should never risk more capital than they can afford to lose in a single trade.

Example: John practices disciplined risk management by limiting each trade to a small percentage of his total capital. This approach shields him from catastrophic losses.

3. Emotional Control:

Emotional discipline is crucial for maintaining composure during periods of drawdowns or market turbulence.

Example: Emily employs meditation techniques and mindfulness exercises to keep her emotions in check, ensuring that fear or greed does not drive her decisions.

4. Consistent Routine:

Establishing a daily trading routine helps reinforce discipline by creating structure and minimizing impulsive actions.

Example: Mike follows a strict daily routine that includes market analysis, trade planning, and review. This disciplined approach keeps him on track and reduces emotional reactions.

5. Review and Adaptation:

Regularly review and adapt your trading plan based on performance and market conditions. Flexibility within the boundaries of discipline is key.

Example: Daniel periodically assesses his trading plan, making adjustments based on lessons learned and changes in market dynamics. This disciplined approach allows him to evolve and adapt.

6. Accountability:

Hold yourself accountable for your actions and decisions. Journaling your trades and decisions can help track your adherence to discipline.

Example: Alex maintains a detailed trading journal that includes notes on his emotions during each trade. This practice holds him accountable for any lapses in discipline.

7. Proper Sleep Routine:

Adequate and consistent sleep is essential for maintaining trading discipline. Lack of sleep can impair cognitive function and emotional control, leading to impulsive decisions.

Example: Jane prioritizes her sleep, ensuring she gets 7-8 hours of rest each night. This helps her stay alert and emotionally balanced during trading hours.

8. Regular Exercise:

Exercise not only benefits physical health but also enhances mental well-being. Regular physical activity can reduce stress, improve focus, and boost self-discipline.

Example: Mark incorporates daily workouts into his routine. The endorphins released during exercise help him manage stress and maintain a disciplined mindset.

9. Healthy Diet:

Nutrition plays a significant role in cognitive function and emotional stability. A balanced diet can provide the energy and mental clarity needed for disciplined trading.

Example: Lisa follows a diet rich in whole grains, fruits, vegetables, and lean proteins. This nutritious diet supports her cognitive function and emotional resilience during trading.

Emphasizing the importance of proper sleep, regular exercise, and a healthy diet highlights the holistic nature of trading discipline. These factors contribute to a trader's overall well-being, which in turn strengthens their ability to adhere to a disciplined trading plan. By maintaining physical and mental health, traders are better equipped to withstand the emotional challenges of the market and make rational decisions with discipline at the forefront.

It is often said "In the journey of trading, discipline outshines intelligence over time."

9: The Power of Patience: Waiting for the Right Options Opportunities

In the fast-paced world of options trading, patience is often the unsung hero that separates the prudent trader from the impulsive speculator. This chapter explores the transformative influence of patience in the realm of options trading, offering valuable insights into how to harness its power for long-term success. We will delve into various aspects of patience, including its role in trading strategy, its impact on decision-making, and practical techniques for developing and maintaining patience as a trader.

Patience as a Trading Virtue:
A. Rational Decision-Making:

Patience empowers traders to approach the market with a clear and rational mindset. It allows them to assess opportunities calmly, weigh risks and rewards, and make informed decisions.

Example: Sarah, a patient trader, waits for her predetermined entry conditions to be met before placing a trade. She refrains from acting on every market fluctuation, ensuring that her decisions are deliberate and rational.

B. Avoiding Impulsive Actions:

Impatience often leads to impulsive actions, such as entering trades hastily, chasing price movements, or ignoring risk management rules. These actions can result in significant losses.

Example: John, driven by impatience and fear of missing out (FOMO), buys call options on a stock without conducting thorough research. The stock experiences a sudden drop, and he ends up losing a substantial portion of his capital.

C. Timing and Opportunity:

Patience is closely tied to timing in options trading. It allows traders to wait for optimal entry and exit points, aligning their strategies with favorable market conditions.

Example: Mike, a patient trader, patiently observes a stock with a strong upward trend. He waits for a temporary price pullback before entering a bullish options trade, ensuring he maximizes his profit potential.

D. Emotional Control:

Patience is a key factor in emotional control. It helps traders avoid emotional reactions to market fluctuations and prevents them from making decisions driven by fear or greed.

Example: Emily, a patient trader, experiences a sharp market downturn. Instead of panicking and selling her positions impulsively, she stays patient and sticks to her well-defined trading plan.

E. Consistency and Longevity:

Traders who prioritize patience tend to have a more consistent and sustainable trading career. They avoid the boom-and-bust cycle often associated with impulsive trading.

Example: Daniel, a patient trader, has been consistently profitable over the years. His patience in waiting for high-probability setups has allowed him to weather market storms and achieve lasting success.

The Waiting Game:
A. Maximizing Probabilities:

Waiting for the right opportunities means entering trades with a higher probability of success. This increases the chances of profitable outcomes and reduces the risk of losses.

Example: Sarah patiently waits for a stock's implied volatility to increase before selling put options. This strategy gives her a better chance of profiting from time decay and falling volatility.

B. Avoiding Low-Probability Trades:

Impatience can lead to entering trades prematurely, even when the odds are stacked against the trader. These low-probability trades often result in losses.

Example: John, driven by impatience, buys call options on a stock without waiting for a clear trend to develop. The stock remains range-bound, and his options expire worthless.

C. Aligning with Market Trends:

Waiting for the right opportunities allows traders to align their strategies with prevailing market trends. It ensures that they aren't swimming against the current.

Example: Mike patiently observes a stock in a strong uptrend. Instead of trading against the trend, he waits for a suitable pullback to join the bullish momentum.

D. Reducing Emotional Stress:

Patience in the waiting game reduces emotional stress. Traders who wait for high-probability setups are less likely to second-guess their decisions or succumb to anxiety.

Example: Emily, with a patient approach, avoids the stress of constantly monitoring the market for short-term opportunities. She waits for the right moments to execute her trades.

E. Protecting Capital:

Waiting for favorable opportunities safeguards trading capital. It prevents impulsive trades that can deplete a trader's account.

Example: Daniel, who practices patience, avoids chasing after every market move. By doing so, he protects his capital from unnecessary risks and potential losses.

F. Embracing Selectivity:

Waiting for the right opportunities encourages traders to be selective in their choices. This selectivity enhances the quality of trades and fosters a disciplined trading approach.

Example: Sarah's patience leads her to carefully evaluate potential trades, filtering out those that don't meet her stringent criteria. This selectivity contributes to her overall success.

Staying Patient in Different Market Conditions:
A. Patience in Bull Markets:

In bull markets, patience may manifest as waiting for pullbacks or consolidations to enter positions at favorable prices.

Example: Mike exercises patience by not chasing after soaring stock prices during a bull market. He waits for minor retracements before considering call option purchases.

B. Patience in Bear Markets:

During bear markets, patience may involve holding onto defensive strategies or positioning for short-selling opportunities.

Example: Emily remains patient in bear markets by holding protective puts on her portfolio, safeguarding against significant losses.

C. Patience in Sideways Markets:

Sideways markets require the patience to tolerate range-bound price movements and to wait for breakout or breakdown signals.

Example: Daniel, in a sideways market, exercises patience by refraining from directional bets and instead employing non-directional strategies like iron condors.

D. Adapting Patience to Different Scenarios:

Recognize Changing Dynamics: Stay attuned to market sentiment, economic factors, and technical indicators to adjust your patience strategy accordingly.

Flexibility in Strategy: Be open to shifting from aggressive strategies to conservative ones or vice versa based on evolving market conditions.

Embrace a Tactical Approach: Consider tactical patience, which may involve shorter holding periods or frequent portfolio rebalancing during certain market phases.

Patience: Trader Case Studies
Trader Story 1: The Transformation - Patience and the Area of Value

Rajesh, an aspiring options trader, embarked on his trading journey with unwavering enthusiasm. He had a basic technical strategy in his arsenal, relying on the interplay between the 20 Exponential Moving Average (EMA) and the 50 EMA. His strategy was simple: buy when the 20 EMA crossed above the 50 EMA and sell when the opposite occurred.

However, Rajesh's initial enthusiasm soon turned into frustration as he encountered a string of losses. Every trade he entered seemed to trigger his stop-loss orders, causing him to lose a substantial portion of his trading capital. Discouraged and disheartened, Rajesh decided to abandon his strategy, hopping from one approach to another with every loss, desperately seeking a winning formula.

Despite his relentless pursuit of the perfect strategy, Rajesh's trading account continued to bleed red, and the losses seemed unending. It was a dark period in his trading journey, one filled with frustration and disappointment.

But then, Rajesh stumbled upon a concept that would forever change his perspective on trading: the "Area of Value." He realized that impatience had been his Achilles' heel all along. He had been entering trades hastily as soon as the 20 EMA crossed above the 50 EMA, without considering the broader context of the market.

The "Area of Value" concept taught Rajesh the importance of patience in trading decisions. Instead of impulsively entering trades, he learned to wait patiently for the market to align with his strategy. Rajesh understood that no matter how tempting the market appeared, he needed to wait until the price pulled back to the area of value, where the odds of a successful trade were significantly higher.

With this newfound wisdom, Rajesh transformed his trading approach. He patiently waited for the market to present opportunities that fit his strategy and entered trades only when the conditions aligned with the concept of the "Area of Value." No longer driven by impatience, he embraced a more disciplined and methodical approach to trading.

Over time, Rajesh's trading career flourished. The losses that had once plagued his account were replaced by consistent profits. By understanding the importance of patience and the concept of the "Area of Value," Rajesh had unlocked the key to successful trading. His journey from frustration to success served as a testament to the transformative power of patience in the world of options trading.

Trader Story 2: Journey to Patience and Profitability

Sourabh, a budding options trader, was eager to conquer the world of finance. His ambition was matched only by his impatience, a trait that would soon become his trading Achilles' heel.

In the early days of his trading career, Sourabh exhibited a peculiar pattern. Every time he entered a trade, fear would grip him within minutes, leading to impulsive decisions to cut the trade at a loss. This fear of further losses haunted him, and it repeated relentlessly until his trading account was severely wounded. He couldn't fathom why this fear seemed to kick in as soon as he entered a trade.

Frustrated and perplexed, Sourabh decided to take a step back and perform some self-awareness. He embarked on a journey to understand the root cause of his impulsive actions and unravel the mystery behind his fear-induced exits.

As Sourabh delved deeper into introspection, a revelation emerged: his position sizing was the culprit. He realized that he had been trading with a position size that was far too large, driven by the hope of making substantial profits in mere minutes. His impatience to become wealthy quickly had led him down a treacherous path.

In a profound moment of realization, Sourabh made a pivotal decision. He opted to reduce his position size to the smallest, acknowledging that his previous approach had magnified his fear and impatience. With smaller positions, he felt less vulnerable to sudden price movements and was no longer consumed by the fear of losing large sums.

As he implemented this change, Sourabh's trading behavior underwent a remarkable transformation. He found that with reduced position sizes, he no longer panicked at the slightest market fluctuation. Instead, he began to ride longer trends and patiently allowed his trades to develop over time.

Despite his position sizes being smaller, Sourabh was making bigger profits than before. By eliminating the negative impact of bad position sizing, he had unleashed the power of patience in his trading. He no longer sought instant wealth but understood the value of consistent, sustainable gains.

Sourabh's trading account began to recover, and over time, it flourished. His journey from impulsive exits and fear-induced decisions to disciplined patience and profitability was a testament to the transformative effect of understanding one's weaknesses and taking decisive actions to rectify them. Sourabh had learned that in the world of options trading, patience could be the difference between failure and success.

Trader Story 3: Journey from Impulsive Losses to Informed Gains

Gopal, a curious individual, had often heard his friends brag about their newfound success in options trading. Seduced by the allure of quick riches, he decided to take the plunge without a second thought. Ignoring the fundamentals of options trading, he promptly invested his hard-earned savings.

As a novice in the complex world of options, Gopal sought refuge in the popular practice of following buy/sell signals from various trading groups. He executed these signals unquestioningly, convinced that easy profits awaited. Unfortunately, his blind reliance on these signals quickly led to a series of devastating losses.

As his trading account dwindled to a fraction of its former self, Gopal found himself in a dire financial predicament. It was a harsh lesson that left him teetering on the edge of despair. But in the depths of his financial turmoil, he stumbled upon a valuable realization – the importance of acquiring knowledge before risking hard-earned money.

Determined to rectify his past mistakes, Gopal embarked on a transformative journey. For six months, he dedicated himself wholly to learning the fundamentals of options trading. He immersed himself in the intricacies of technical analysis, delved deep into the psychology of trading, and honed his skills through rigorous paper trading.

Gopal's relentless pursuit of knowledge changed his perspective entirely. Armed with a newfound understanding of the market, he re-entered the world of real trading. But this time, he approached it with patience and prudence. He no longer sought shortcuts to quick riches but embraced the journey of consistent learning and disciplined trading.

The results of Gopal's transformation were nothing short of remarkable. He started earning profits consistently, his account balance grew steadily, and the financial hardships that once loomed over him became a distant memory.

Gopal's journey was a testament to the transformative power of patience and education in options trading. By recognizing the folly of impulsive decisions and dedicating himself to learning the ropes, he had not only salvaged his financial well-being but had also discovered a fulfilling and sustainable path to success in the intricate world of options trading.

Trader Story 4: Breaking Free from Compulsive Trading

Kuldeep, an avid intraday trader of options, was no stranger to the ups and downs of the financial markets. His trading journey had seen its fair share of profits and losses, but one fateful day would reveal a critical flaw in his approach.

On this particular day, Kuldeep received news of a devastating loss within his family—a close cousin had passed away. Emotions ran high, and the weight of sorrow hung heavily over him. The timing was particularly unfortunate, as it was also an expiry day for options trading.

Despite the profound grief that enveloped him, Kuldeep couldn't resist the alluring pull of the market. He found himself constantly sneaking glances at his phone, tracking the movements of stocks and options. Whenever a family member approached, he hastily concealed his phone, torn between his responsibilities and his trading impulses.

In the midst of this emotional turmoil, Kuldeep decided to take a long position in Bank Nifty call options. However, one of his elderly aunts engaged him in a conversation that seemed to stretch on for an eternity—15 minutes that felt like an eternity in the world of intraday trading.

Once the conversation finally concluded, Kuldeep rushed to a secluded spot to check his trading account, only to be met with a heart-wrenching sight—a substantial loss. It was a harsh awakening for Kuldeep, who realized that his impatience and compulsive trading habits had exacted a hefty toll on his financial well-being.

In the wake of this painful experience, Kuldeep resolved to undergo a profound transformation. He recognized the urgent need for patience and discipline in his trading journey. He decided to draft a trading holiday plan for himself, vowing not to trade on special days, during family gatherings, or in the midst of emotionally charged situations.

Kuldeep's newfound commitment to discipline and patience bore fruit over time. He learned to prioritize his family and emotional well-being over impulsive trading decisions. By allowing himself the space to step back during significant life events, he not only preserved his capital but also found solace in knowing that true wealth extended far beyond the confines of the trading screen.

10: Psychology of Loss: Coping with Drawdowns and Recovering

Understanding the Emotional Impact of Loss

The Emotional Rollercoaster of Trading Losses:

The world of trading is a tumultuous journey where emotions often ride a rollercoaster. When traders face losses, a wide spectrum of emotions engulfs them, each vying for dominance in the trader's mind. These emotions include:

Fear: Perhaps the most prevalent emotion, fear grips traders when they realize they are losing money. Fear of financial ruin, fear of failure, and fear of being wrong can become paralyzing, leading to irrational decisions.

Frustration: Trading losses can trigger a sense of frustration, especially when a trade doesn't go as planned despite careful analysis. Traders may feel powerless or unable to control outcomes, fueling their frustration.

Self-Doubt: Losses can erode a trader's confidence in their abilities. Self-doubt creeps in, making them question their strategies, skills, and even their decision to trade in the first place.

Anger: It's not uncommon for traders to feel anger towards themselves, the market, or external factors. This anger can cloud judgment and lead to impulsive actions.

Guilt: Traders sometimes experience guilt, particularly when they have invested family savings or retirement funds. Guilt stems from the sense of responsibility for risking these assets.

Desperate Hope: Traders may also cling to a desperate hope when facing losses. This irrational hope manifests when they refuse to cut their losses, holding onto a losing position in the futile belief that it will somehow turn around in their favor. This hope-driven behavior can transform manageable losses into devastating ones.

To illustrate the psychological toll of drawdowns, let's delve into a trader's story:

The Fear of Losing Everything

Meet Sarah, an experienced trader who had built a substantial trading portfolio over the years. She was well-versed in market analysis and had a strong track record of profitable trades. However, a series of unfortunate events led to a significant drawdown in her portfolio.

As Sarah's losses mounted, fear began to grip her. The fear of losing everything she had worked so hard to accumulate was paralyzing. She could hardly sleep, constantly checking her trading account in the middle of the night. Her analysis became clouded, and she started making impulsive decisions to recoup her losses.

Sarah's experience is a stark example of how the fear of losing one's trading capital can have a paralyzing effect on decision-making. It can lead traders to abandon their well-thought-out strategies, chase high-risk opportunities, and make irrational choices in a desperate attempt to avoid further losses.

Understanding these emotional responses and their impact is crucial for traders on their journey to cope with losses and emerge as more resilient and disciplined participants in the financial markets.

Common Responses to Trading Losses
Denial and Avoidance

Trading losses can trigger various responses, and one of the most common is the instinct to deny or avoid acknowledging those losses. This coping mechanism can have severe consequences for traders, as it prevents them from taking necessary actions to mitigate the damage.

The Denial Reflex: Some traders find it incredibly challenging to accept that they are incurring losses. They may convince themselves that the losses aren't real or that the market will eventually correct in their favor. This denial reflex is an attempt to shield themselves from the emotional pain of facing the reality of their losses.

Avoiding Account Statements: Traders who are deep in denial may avoid looking at their trading account statements altogether. They might refuse to log in to their trading platforms or conveniently "forget" their login credentials, essentially burying their heads in the sand.

Hiding from Loved Ones: In extreme cases, traders may even hide their losses from loved ones, fearing judgment or disappointment. They might take desperate measures to conceal their financial losses, which can lead to strained relationships and a deeper sense of isolation.

To illustrate the dangerous path of denial and avoidance, let's explore the story of Alex:

Alex's Denial and Isolation

Alex was an avid options trader who had experienced consistent success in the past. However, a sudden market downturn led to substantial losses in his portfolio. Unable to accept these losses, Alex resorted to denial and avoidance.

He convinced himself that the market turbulence was temporary and that his losses were merely paper losses that would eventually rebound. In the meantime, he stopped checking his trading account, avoiding the reality of his deteriorating financial situation.

Alex's isolation grew as he distanced himself from his trading friends and mentors. He stopped attending trading forums and chat groups, afraid that discussing his losses would make them real. He even withdrew from social gatherings, preferring to maintain the façade of success.

Over time, Alex's losses deepened, but his denial persisted. By the time he finally confronted his losses, they had snowballed into an insurmountable financial burden. His isolation had also taken a toll on his mental well-being, compounding the emotional impact of his losses.

Chasing Losses

Another common response to trading losses is the perilous pursuit of recovering those losses through impulsive and high-risk trades. Traders caught in the trap of chasing losses often abandon their well-considered strategies and risk management rules in a desperate attempt to claw back their losses.

Reckless Trading Decisions: Chasing losses can lead traders to make irrational decisions. They might increase their position sizes, trade assets they are unfamiliar with, or engage in highly leveraged trades, all in the hope of recouping their losses quickly.

The Vicious Cycle: Unfortunately, this approach often results in compounding losses. The emotional turmoil caused by each new loss drives traders to take even greater risks in subsequent trades, creating a vicious cycle of desperation and financial devastation.

Consequences of Chasing Losses: Traders who chase losses may find themselves in deeper financial trouble than they originally faced. The consequences can include depleting their trading capital, incurring substantial debt, and suffering severe emotional distress.

To illustrate the dangers of chasing losses, consider the story of Sarah:

Sarah's Downward Spiral

Sarah was a seasoned trader with a history of successful trading strategies. However, a string of unexpected losses shook her confidence. In a desperate bid to recover her losses, she abandoned her tried-and-true methods and started taking reckless risks.

Sarah increased her position sizes dramatically and ventured into unfamiliar markets. She engaged in margin trading to amplify her potential gains, but this also amplified her potential losses. The more losses she incurred, the riskier her trades became.

As Sarah's losses continued to mount, she became trapped in a downward spiral of desperation. She was chasing losses, believing that a single big win would make everything right. However, this pursuit only led her deeper into financial ruin.

Losing Confidence in Financial Markets and Quitting

Another significant response to trading losses is the loss of confidence in the financial markets and, ultimately, the decision to quit trading altogether. This response can have a lasting impact on a trader's financial well-being and their perception of the trading world.

Emotional Toll: Suffering substantial losses can take a significant emotional toll on traders. They may question their ability to navigate the markets successfully and start to view trading as an insurmountable challenge.

Doubting the System: Some traders might begin to doubt the fairness or integrity of the financial markets. They may wonder if the markets are rigged against retail traders or if they are simply not cut out for the world of trading.

Negative Self-Image: The experience of losses can also lead to a negative self-image. Traders may perceive themselves as failures or as individuals incapable of achieving success in the trading arena.

The Decision to Quit: When traders reach a point where they believe that trading is causing more harm than good, they might decide to quit. This decision can be accompanied by feelings of relief, but it can also bring about a sense of regret for not having been able to overcome the challenges.

To illustrate this topic, consider the story of Emma:

Emma's Crisis of Confidence

Emma had been trading for several years and had built a successful track record. However, a series of unexpected market events led to significant losses in her portfolio. The emotional toll of these losses was overwhelming.

As Emma's losses mounted, she began to lose confidence in her ability to read the markets and make profitable trades. She questioned the fairness of the financial system and felt as though the markets were conspiring against her.

The negative self-image that developed during this period further eroded her confidence. Emma saw herself as a failure, unable to bounce back from her losses. She started to believe that trading was a futile endeavor for someone like her.

Ultimately, Emma made the difficult decision to quit trading altogether. While this decision brought relief from the emotional turmoil she had been experiencing, it also carried a sense of regret for not persevering through the challenging times.

Strategies for Coping with Drawdowns
Acceptance and Emotional Resilience

Trading losses are an inherent part of the trading journey, and learning to accept them is crucial for a trader's emotional well-being and long-term success. In this section, we delve into strategies that can help traders cope with drawdowns more effectively and build emotional resilience.

1. Acceptance as a Cornerstone: Accepting that losses are an integral part of trading is a fundamental step. Traders should acknowledge that even the most successful professionals experience drawdowns. It's not a matter of if losses will occur but when.

2. Embracing Emotional Resilience: Emotional resilience is the ability to bounce back from setbacks, and it's a skill that can be cultivated. Traders can enhance their emotional resilience through practices such as mindfulness, meditation, and cognitive reframing. These techniques enable traders to manage stress and anxiety during challenging times.

3. Journaling and Self-Reflection: Keeping a trading journal is a powerful tool for both accepting losses and building emotional resilience. Traders can document their trades, emotions, and thoughts. Regular self-reflection helps traders recognize patterns in their behavior and develop strategies for improving decision-making.

To illustrate the importance of acceptance and emotional resilience, consider the story of Daniel:

Daniel's Journey to Acceptance

Daniel, an experienced trader, had enjoyed years of profitable trading. However, a series of unexpected market events led to a significant drawdown in his portfolio. At first, he resisted accepting the losses, clinging to the hope that the market would turn in his favor.

As days turned into weeks, Daniel's emotional turmoil grew. He found himself unable to focus on new trading opportunities, and anxiety and self-doubt crept in. It was only when he began practicing mindfulness meditation that he started to accept his losses as part of the trading process.

Through meditation and self-reflection, Daniel learned to detach himself emotionally from his trades. He recognized that losses were an intrinsic aspect of trading and that resisting them only exacerbated his emotional distress. With a newfound sense of acceptance, he was able to move forward, learning from his losses and ultimately improving his trading strategies.

Risk Management and Position Sizing

Effective risk management is paramount in mitigating the impact of trading losses. In this part, we explore strategies for managing risk and position sizing to protect capital during drawdowns.

4. Diversification: Spreading risk across different asset classes or trading strategies can reduce the impact of a drawdown on a trader's overall portfolio. Diversification can help safeguard capital during turbulent market periods.

5. Setting Stop-Loss Orders: Placing stop-loss orders is a critical risk management technique. Traders should determine their risk tolerance and set stop-loss levels accordingly. These orders can help limit losses and prevent emotional decision-making.

6. Adjusting Position Sizes: During drawdowns, traders should consider reducing their position sizes to preserve capital. Smaller positions mean that losses have a less significant impact on the overall portfolio, allowing traders to weather challenging periods more effectively.

To illustrate the significance of risk management and position sizing, let's look at the story of Maria:

Maria's Risk-Managed Recovery

Maria had been a diligent trader, meticulously managing her risk and position sizes. However, a series of unexpected market events resulted in a drawdown in her portfolio. Rather than chasing losses or abandoning her risk management principles, Maria chose to adjust her position sizes and limit her exposure to risk.

By reducing her position sizes and setting tighter stop-loss orders, Maria protected her remaining capital. This allowed her to weather the drawdown without the emotional distress that often accompanies significant losses. Over time, as market conditions improved, Maria was able to gradually increase her position sizes and rebuild her portfolio.

Recovering from Drawdowns
Assessing and Learning from Losses

Recovering from trading losses is a crucial phase in a trader's journey. In this section, we explore strategies that help traders assess their losses and extract valuable lessons from each drawdown, ensuring that they evolve as more resilient and informed traders.

1. Post-Mortem Analysis: After experiencing a drawdown, traders should conduct a post-mortem analysis of their trades. This involves a comprehensive review of each trade, including entry and exit points, risk management strategies, and emotional responses during the trade. By dissecting their trades, traders can pinpoint where mistakes were made.

2. Identifying Patterns: Traders should look for recurring patterns in their losses. Are there common triggers that lead to drawdowns? Identifying these patterns can help traders address underlying issues in their trading strategies or behavior.

3. Learning from Mistakes: Every loss provides an opportunity to learn and improve. Traders should focus on the lessons they can extract from each drawdown. These lessons may relate to risk management, strategy adjustments, or emotional discipline.

To illustrate the importance of assessing and learning from losses, consider the story of Rachel:

Rachel's Journey of Self-Improvement

Rachel had been an active trader for years, but a significant drawdown shook her confidence. Instead of succumbing to despair, she chose to embark on a journey of self-improvement.

Rachel meticulously reviewed her recent trades, taking note of her decision-making process and emotional responses. She identified a pattern of impulsive trading during moments of heightened market volatility. This realization prompted her to work on her emotional discipline and to implement stricter risk management rules.

By learning from her mistakes and addressing her emotional triggers, Rachel was able to gradually rebuild her trading strategy. Over time, she found herself making more calculated decisions and regaining her lost confidence.

Rebuilding Confidence

The process of rebuilding confidence after a drawdown is essential for a trader's long-term success. It involves not only addressing the technical aspects of trading but also the psychological aspects.

4. Incremental Progress: Traders should focus on making incremental progress rather than expecting an immediate return to previous levels of profitability. Setting achievable goals and milestones can help rebuild confidence step by step.

5. Paper Trading: For traders who have experienced significant drawdowns and are struggling to regain confidence, paper trading can be a valuable tool. It allows them to practice without risking real capital, rebuild their skills, and rebuild their confidence.

6. Seek Support: Seeking support from mentors or joining trading communities can provide a sense of camaraderie and valuable

insights. Knowing that others have faced similar challenges and successfully rebuilt their confidence can be motivating.

7. Taking a Break

A break from trading after a drawdown offers traders a chance to rest, recover, and gain perspective. It helps prevent impulsive decisions driven by the desire to recoup losses quickly and allows traders to detox from emotional stress. This period of rejuvenation promotes mental clarity, self-awareness, and a healthier mindset, ultimately contributing to more effective and disciplined trading when they return to the markets.

To illustrate the process of rebuilding confidence, let's look at the story of Mark:

Mark's Gradual Comeback

Mark had a thriving trading career until a severe drawdown left him feeling defeated. He decided to take a break from live trading and, instead, focused on paper trading to regain his confidence.

During this period, Mark set achievable goals for himself, aiming for consistent profitability in his paper trading account. He also sought guidance from experienced traders who had faced similar setbacks.

Over time, Mark's confidence began to return as he saw positive results in his paper trading efforts. He gradually transitioned back to live trading, starting with smaller positions to manage risk effectively. Through patience and persistence, Mark not only recovered his lost confidence but also continued to build on it, ultimately achieving greater success than before.

11: Trading with Conviction: Building Confidence

Understanding Your Trading Style

One of the fundamental steps towards building confidence in your strategies is understanding your trading style. Your trading style defines how you interact with the markets, and it plays a significant role in shaping your overall approach to trading. In this section, we'll explore the importance of defining and aligning with your trading style.

Defining Your Trading Style:

Trading styles can be as diverse as the traders themselves. Here, we'll outline some of the common trading styles to help you identify your preferred approach:

Day Trading: Day traders open and close positions within the same trading day. They focus on short-term price movements and aim to profit from intraday fluctuations.

Swing Trading: Swing traders hold positions for several days to weeks, capitalizing on medium-term price trends. They often rely on technical analysis to identify entry and exit points.

Position Trading: Position traders have a long-term perspective, holding trades for weeks, months, or even years. They typically focus on fundamental analysis and macroeconomic trends.

Scalping: Scalpers aim to profit from small price movements, executing numerous trades throughout the day. Speed and precision are essential for scalping.

Algorithmic Trading: Algorithmic traders employ automated systems and algorithms to execute trades based on predefined criteria. This style requires significant technical expertise.

To identify your preferred trading style, consider your goals, risk tolerance, available time, and emotional disposition. Do you thrive in fast-paced, short-term trades, or are you more comfortable with a patient, long-term approach? Understanding your trading style is the first step in building confidence in your strategies.

Aligning with Personality:

Your personality traits and preferences play a crucial role in determining your trading style. Here's how:

Risk Tolerance: Are you risk-averse or risk-tolerant? Your comfort level with risk will influence your choice of trading style. For example, day trading can be riskier due to its short-term nature, while long-term investing tends to be less volatile.

Patience: Consider your natural patience level. Day trading requires quick decision-making and constant monitoring, while long-term investing allows for a more relaxed approach.

Analytical Skills: Reflect on your analytical abilities. Swing trading and day trading often involve technical analysis, requiring strong analytical skills, whereas long-term investing may rely more on fundamental analysis.

Emotional Resilience: Think about how well you handle stress and uncertainty. Scalping can be emotionally intense due to its fast pace, while position trading allows for a calmer experience.

Lifestyle: Your daily routine and commitments also matter. If you have a full-time job, day trading may be challenging, whereas swing trading or long-term investing might align better with your lifestyle.

Picking up your trading style is important, being consistent with it is equally important not to make impulsive trades

Time Frame Consistency:

Consistency in your chosen time frame is paramount for building familiarity and confidence in your trading strategies. Here's why it matters:

Specialization: Focusing on a specific time frame allows you to develop expertise in the strategies and patterns associated with that frame. You become attuned to the nuances of the market within your chosen time horizon.

Psychological Comfort: Consistency in your time frame reduces cognitive load and emotional strain. You become accustomed to the pace and rhythm of your chosen trading style, enhancing your decision-making process.

Improved Analysis: When you consistently trade within a particular time frame, you can refine your technical and fundamental analysis to better suit that frame. This enables you to identify opportunities and manage risks more effectively.

Evaluation: Over time, you can evaluate the performance of your strategies within your chosen time frame. This helps you fine-tune your approach, identify strengths and weaknesses, and build confidence in your trading abilities.

Becoming self-aware of your personality traits and preferences is crucial for selecting a trading style that suits you best. A harmonious match between your trading style and your personality traits will lead to more confident and successful trading decisions. In the next sections, we'll explore further steps to strengthen your conviction in your options trading strategies, building upon this understanding of your trading style.

Less is more

In the vast landscape of financial markets, it can be tempting for options traders to cast a wide net, seeking opportunities across numerous securities and instruments. However, one essential principle that often leads to greater confidence in trading is the concept of quality over quantity. In this section, we'll explore the advantages of narrowing down your list of securities to trade and how this approach can contribute to a more confident trading experience.

Quality Over Quantity:

The concept of "less is more" can be particularly apt when it comes to options trading. While the financial markets offer a multitude of securities, focusing on a smaller, carefully chosen set of assets can be advantageous for several reasons:

In-Depth Knowledge: Concentrating your attention on a limited number of securities allows you to develop a deeper understanding of each one. You can become well-versed in their historical price patterns, volatility tendencies, and the factors that influence their movements. This in-depth knowledge is essential for making informed trading decisions.

Thorough Research: A narrower focus enables you to conduct more thorough research on the securities in your portfolio. You can dedicate time to analyze financial reports, news, and relevant market data specific to your chosen assets. This research empowers you to identify potential trading opportunities and assess their risks with greater precision.

Effective Risk Management: Managing risk is a critical aspect of options trading. When you trade a smaller pool of securities, you can more effectively manage your risk exposure. By understanding the unique characteristics of each asset, you can tailor your risk management strategies to suit their individual profiles.

Confidence Building: As you become intimately familiar with your selected securities, you naturally build confidence in your ability to predict their price movements and execute successful trades. This confidence is grounded in knowledge and research, reducing the likelihood of impulsive or emotionally-driven decisions.

Time Efficiency: Focusing on fewer securities also translates to better time management. Instead of spreading your efforts thinly across numerous assets, you can allocate your time and resources more efficiently to conduct in-depth analysis and execute well-considered trades.

Process, Not Outcome

When it comes to options trading, it's natural to fixate on the outcome of each trade. After all, the ultimate goal is to make profitable trades. However, in this section, we'll explore a vital concept that can significantly enhance your confidence in trading: understanding that the process is often more critical than the immediate outcome.

Outcome vs. Process:

Many traders tend to judge their success solely based on the immediate results of their trades. Winning trades are celebrated, while losing trades can be deeply frustrating. While it's essential to have profitable trades, overly focusing on individual outcomes can lead to anxiety, impulsive decision-making, and a lack of long-term confidence.

Instead, consider shifting your perspective. Acknowledge that trading is inherently uncertain, and no one can predict the outcome of every trade with absolute certainty. Therefore, concentrating on the quality and consistency of your trading process can be far more valuable.

Continuous Improvement:

By emphasizing the importance of the trading process, you can achieve several benefits that contribute to your confidence:

Learning Opportunities: Regardless of whether a trade ends in profit or loss, each trade offers an opportunity for learning and growth. Analyzing the process behind every trade allows you to identify what went well and what could be improved. Over time, this leads to a deeper understanding of your trading strategies and a more refined approach.

Reduced Emotional Impact: When you recognize that losses are an inevitable part of trading and that they can occur even with a well-executed process, you'll be better equipped to manage emotions. This reduces the emotional rollercoaster that often accompanies trading and fosters emotional resilience.

Long-Term Focus: Trading is not a sprint but a marathon. A myopic focus on individual trade outcomes can lead to impatience and anxiety. On the other hand, concentrating on the process encourages a long-term perspective, where consistent execution of a well-defined strategy is valued over the course of many trades.

Confidence Building: Over time, as you fine-tune your trading process based on continuous improvement, you'll naturally gain more confidence in your abilities. This confidence stems from your understanding of the robustness of your approach, rather than short-term gains or losses.

Confidence: Trader Case Studies

Trader Story: Benny's Journey from Day Trading Back to Confidence

Benny had always been a meticulous and disciplined trader. For years, he had followed a positional trading strategy that had brought him consistent profits and a sense of financial security. However, as time went on, he couldn't help but notice the allure of day trading.

The idea of making quick, intraday profits was tantalizing, and Benny found himself increasingly drawn to the fast-paced world of day trading. He believed that if he could become a successful day trader, he could potentially multiply his earnings in no time.

With this ambition in mind, Benny decided to dip his toes into day trading while maintaining his full-time job. He started opening and closing trades within the same trading day, trying to capitalize on short-term market movements. But as he delved deeper into day trading, he encountered a series of challenges he had never experienced before.

The emotional rollercoaster of day trading hit Benny hard. The stress of monitoring the markets throughout the workday and making quick decisions took a toll on his mental and emotional well-being. He found himself second-guessing every trade, and his anxiety levels soared.

In addition to his emotional struggles, Benny's full-time job left him with limited time and focus for day trading. He often had to rush his trading decisions, leading to impulsive and ill-considered trades. The pressure of juggling both his job and day trading began to affect his performance and erode his confidence.

After several months of day trading, Benny decided to take a step back and evaluate his trading journey. He meticulously reviewed his trading history, analyzing both his successes and losses. What he discovered was a clear pattern – his positional trading had consistently generated profits, while day trading had led to a series of losses.

It was a sobering realization for Benny. He understood that day trading didn't align with his personal traits, lifestyle, or emotional resilience. Instead of trying to force himself into a trading style that didn't suit him, he made a pivotal decision to return to his tried-and-true positional trading approach.

With renewed focus and a regained sense of confidence, Benny reimmersed himself in positional trading. He recognized that success in trading wasn't solely about chasing quick profits but about finding a strategy that matched his strengths and personality.

As the months passed, Benny's confidence grew along with his profits. He learned a valuable lesson about the importance of trading within one's comfort zone and embracing a style that suits individual traits. Benny's journey from day trading back to positional trading was a testament to the power of self-awareness and the significance of maintaining confidence in one's trading path.

Trader Story 2: Transition from Volatility to Confidence

Rajesh was no stranger to the world of trading. For years, he had carved out a successful niche for himself by trading NIFTY50 options using the iron condor strategy. Month after month, he executed his trades with precision, made small adjustments when necessary, and consistently ended up with profits. It was a formula that had served him well, and Rajesh had grown confident in his trading abilities.

However, as Rajesh continued to explore the intricacies of the financial markets, he couldn't help but notice another trading opportunity that seemed too tempting to pass up – BANKNIFTY. The allure of this index was its higher volatility, which often translated to higher options premiums. Rajesh believed that by switching his trading focus to BANKNIFTY, he could potentially collect even more premium and significantly boost his profits.

With this idea in mind, Rajesh made the bold decision to transition from trading NIFTY50 options to BANKNIFTY options. He believed that his expertise in the iron condor strategy would translate seamlessly to this new asset. However, he was in for a surprise.

BANKNIFTY, true to its reputation, proved to be a much more volatile and unpredictable beast compared to NIFTY50. Price swings were wild, and options prices frequently soared to new heights. Rajesh found himself in unfamiliar territory, as the strategies that had worked so well for him with NIFTY50 did not yield the same results in this new environment.

As Rajesh began trading BANKNIFTY options, he experienced a rollercoaster of emotions he hadn't encountered in a long time. The heightened volatility triggered bouts of anxiety and uncertainty. He attempted to apply the same small adjustment trades that had served him well with NIFTY50 but found that BANKNIFTY's erratic behavior often outpaced his ability to react.

Before long, Rajesh was facing significant losses in his trading account – a situation he had rarely encountered while trading NIFTY50. It was a humbling experience that shook his confidence to the core.

In the midst of this turmoil, Rajesh decided to take a step back and evaluate his choices. He realized that, despite the allure of higher premiums, he had ventured into a trading environment that didn't align with his risk tolerance and emotional resilience. It was a moment of clarity that led him to a crucial decision.

Rajesh chose to return to trading NIFTY50 options, the asset he understood best and was most comfortable with. It was a pragmatic choice that allowed him to regain his confidence and emotional equilibrium. Rajesh recognized that trading wasn't just about chasing premiums or volatility; it was about finding a strategy and asset that matched his personality, risk tolerance, and experience.

As he resumed trading NIFTY50 options, Rajesh felt a renewed sense of confidence and control. He understood that true success in trading came from self-awareness and the ability to recognize when to stay the course and when to adapt. Rajesh's journey from volatility to confidence was a valuable lesson in the importance of trading within one's comfort zone and maintaining unwavering confidence in one's abilities.

12. The Social Aspect of Trading: Dealing with Peer Pressure and Opinions

The Influence of Peer Pressure

Peer pressure in trading can manifest in various forms, and understanding these sources of influence is essential for traders looking to make informed decisions. In this section, we'll delve into different forms of peer pressure in trading and how they wield their impact on trading decisions.

1. Trading Communities:

Trading communities are online or offline groups where traders come together to discuss market trends, share strategies, and provide support. While these communities can be valuable for networking and learning, they also exert peer pressure in several ways:

Herd Mentality: Traders within a community often follow the crowd, imitating the actions of others without conducting independent research. This herd mentality can lead to impulsive trading decisions driven by the fear of missing out or the desire to conform to the group.

Confirmation Bias: In trading communities, individuals tend to seek information and opinions that align with their existing beliefs. This confirmation bias can reinforce groupthink and hinder critical thinking.

Overtrading: When traders witness their peers boasting about profits, it can create pressure to trade frequently and aggressively, potentially leading to overtrading and increased risk exposure.

2. News Channels and Financial Media:

News channels and financial media platforms play a significant role in shaping traders' perceptions and influencing their decisions. Here's how they exert peer pressure:

Sensationalism: Media outlets often sensationalize market events, highlighting extreme price movements and dramatic narratives. Traders exposed to such content may feel compelled to act impulsively based on fear or greed.

Expert Opinions: Financial pundits and analysts on news channels are seen as experts, and their recommendations can sway traders. Following expert advice without conducting independent analysis can result in poor decisions.

Fear of Missing Out (FOMO): Media reports of others' successful trades can induce FOMO, prompting traders to enter positions hastily without proper analysis.

Overreacting to News: Traders influenced by news often overreact to short-term developments, leading to impulsive trades and emotional decisions. Most traders think news triggers price movements, but it's the other way around, price movements are justified by random news.

3. Social Media:

Social media platforms have become prominent channels for traders to share their strategies, successes, and failures. Peer pressure on social media can manifest as:

Comparative Analysis: Traders often compare their performance to others on social media, which can lead to feelings of inadequacy or the need to take excessive risks to match perceived success.

Viral Trading Trends: Social media platforms can propel certain trading trends or stocks into the spotlight. Traders may feel compelled to join the trend, even if it doesn't align with their strategy.

Groupthink and Echo Chambers: Like trading communities, social media can foster groupthink and echo chambers, where traders reinforce each other's opinions without critical analysis.

4. Financial Forums and Chat Rooms:

Online forums and chat rooms dedicated to financial discussions are platforms where traders exchange ideas, tips, and opinions. Peer pressure in these spaces can take various forms:

Hot Stock Picks: Traders may encounter enthusiastic recommendations for specific stocks or options in these forums, leading to impulsive trading decisions.

Echo Chambers: Similar to social media, financial forums can become echo chambers where group consensus drives decisions, potentially disregarding diverse viewpoints.

Fear of Criticism: Traders may hesitate to share their contrarian views in these forums due to fear of criticism or ridicule, leading them to conform to the group's consensus.

5. Analyst Reports and Recommendations:

Financial analysts and research firms frequently release reports and recommendations on various assets. Traders can be influenced by these reports in the following ways:

Confirmation Bias: Traders might give more weight to analyst reports that confirm their existing positions or biases, potentially leading to confirmation bias in decision-making.

Following the Herd: If a widely followed analyst recommends a particular trade, it can lead to a surge of traders taking similar positions without conducting independent analysis.

Ratings Changes: Upgrades or downgrades by prominent analysts can create momentum in a stock or option. Traders may feel compelled to follow these changes, sometimes to their detriment.

Optimizing External Influence
1. Optimal Use of Trading Communities/Social Media/Chat Rooms:

Trading communities serve as dynamic forums for traders to exchange knowledge, strategies, and experiences. When harnessed effectively, these communities can significantly benefit traders. Here's an in-depth look at the optimal use of trading communities:

Selective Engagement: The first step in maximizing the benefits of trading communities is to be selective. Traders should seek out communities that align with their specific trading style and objectives. This selective approach ensures that the information, discussions, and strategies shared within the community are directly relevant to their trading goals. It's crucial to emphasize that traders should never blindly conform to groupthink or adopt strategies that don't align with their personal trading philosophy. Instead, they should critically evaluate the content shared within the community and cherry-pick what suits their trading style. Completely disengaging and focusing on your trading plan is the easiest way out.

Verification of Information: While trading communities can be treasure troves of insights, traders must exercise due diligence in verifying information. They should be cautious about accepting any piece of advice or strategy at face value. Encourage traders to independently verify information they gather from these communities. Stress the importance of cross-referencing facts and figures with other credible sources and conducting their own research before integrating new elements into their trading plans. This critical approach ensures that traders make informed decisions based on a well-rounded understanding of the market.

Contributing Positively: Active participation in trading communities not only allows traders to tap into collective wisdom but also offers opportunities for personal growth. Encourage traders to contribute positively to these communities by sharing their experiences, insights, and trade analyses. Emphasize the value of constructive discussions that promote learning and growth. However, it's essential to caution traders against offering unsolicited advice or imposing their views on others. Instead, suggest that they share their perspectives based on their own experiences, allowing fellow community members to make their independent decisions. Positive contributions enhance the sense of community, foster mutual respect, and create an environment where traders can collectively thrive.

2. Optimal Use of News Channels and Financial Media:

News channels and financial media outlets are integral parts of the trading landscape, offering a wealth of information, analysis, and insights. However, it's essential for traders to approach these sources with a discerning eye to maximize their benefits while avoiding potential pitfalls. Here's a comprehensive look at the optimal use of news channels and financial media:

Diversify Sources: The first step in effectively utilizing news channels and financial media is to diversify information sources. Traders should avoid relying solely on one news outlet or channel. Instead, they should access information from multiple reputable sources. This diverse approach ensures that traders receive a well-rounded perspective on market events, reducing the risk of skewed viewpoints or missing critical insights. Encourage traders to explore a variety of sources, including established news agencies, financial publications, and reputable websites, to gain a broader understanding of market dynamics.

Time Management: While staying informed is essential, traders should also practice effective time management when engaging with news channels and financial media. Overconsumption of news can lead to information overload, anxiety, and impulsive decision-making. Advise traders to allocate specific times for consuming news and market updates. Stress the importance of maintaining a balanced approach by limiting the time spent on news consumption and focusing on quality rather than quantity. This approach ensures that traders stay informed without being overwhelmed by the constant stream of information. Completely avoiding news and focusing on your trading plan and technical analysis is the easiest way out.

Critical Evaluation: Critical evaluation of media content is a fundamental skill for traders. They should approach news and financial analysis with a healthy dose of skepticism, recognizing that media outlets may have their own biases and agendas. Encourage traders to question the sources of information, assess the credibility of analysts and experts, and consider potential biases in the content they consume. By developing a critical mindset, traders can filter out sensationalism and misinformation, making more informed trading decisions. Additionally, suggest that traders seek out balanced perspectives that present multiple sides of an issue to foster a well-informed assessment.

3. Optimal Use of Analyst Reports and Recommendations:

Analyst reports and recommendations play a pivotal role in shaping trading decisions. This section provides traders with valuable insights into:

Objective Evaluation: Traders are urged to approach analyst reports and recommendations with a critical mindset. The emphasis lies in the importance of assessing these reports objectively rather than unquestionably adhering to provided recommendations. The goal is to empower traders to make informed choices based on their own analysis and judgment, even when presented with expert opinions.

Diverse Sources: It is encouraged that traders diversify their sources of analyst reports and recommendations. Relying on insights from various analysts or firms offers a more comprehensive view of the market landscape. This broader perspective can help traders make well-rounded decisions and avoid being overly influenced by a single source.

Accountability: Traders are reminded that, ultimately, they bear the responsibility for their trading outcomes. Regardless of external recommendations, the final decision lies with the trader. This section reinforces the idea that accountability for each trade rests with the individual, emphasizing the need to take ownership of their decisions and their consequences.

Peer-Pressure: Trader Case Studies

Trader Story 1: The News-Driven Gamble

Abdul was no different from many others working a typical 9 to 5 job. He yearned for more in life, and that yearning led him to explore options trading as a way to supplement his fixed income. He envisioned himself as a shrewd trader who would capitalize on the latest news, gaining an edge over the market.

His strategy was straightforward—constantly monitor the live financial news channels and pounce on any breaking news related to securities. Abdul believed that being among the first to react to news would guarantee him a profitable advantage.

One day, his moment arrived when a headline flashed across the screen: "MD of Leading Bank Resigns." Without a second thought, Abdul jumped into action. He invested a substantial portion of his savings in put options, convinced that this was his golden ticket. After all, what could be worse for a bank's stock than the resignation of its Managing Director?

To his astonishment, the stock hardly budged, ending the day with a slight gain. Abdul held onto his put options overnight, thinking that the market would surely react the next day. But when the stock market opened, the reality hit him like a freight train—his losses were staggering.

Confused and disheartened, Abdul wondered why the stock had not plummeted as expected. Perhaps the market had already factored in the MD's resignation, or maybe it wasn't as bad news as he initially thought. Perhaps a more capable leader was taking the helm. It was a sobering moment of realization.

Abdul had learned the hard way that trading the news was no guaranteed path to profits. Countless others had tried it, and the market was far more unpredictable than he had imagined. He found himself in deep financial trouble but refused to be defeated.

With perseverance and a newfound respect for the complexities of trading, Abdul slowly recovered from his losses over the course of a year. He returned to a more balanced life, trading casually and avoiding the pitfalls of overreliance on news.

Trader Story 2: "The Rollercoaster of Investment Decisions"

Meet Kiran, a diligent investor who had poured his life savings into the Indian stock market. He had placed his bets on a NIFTY50 Exchange-Traded Fund (ETF) and had a consistent strategy of selling out-of-the-money (OTM) CALL options. This approach had served him well, allowing him to gradually grow his trading account over time.

Kiran's strategy was simple—he sold OTM CALL options month after month, regardless of market fluctuations. Sometimes the market dipped, and sometimes it surged, but Kiran remained committed to his strategy, steadily increasing his trading account.

One day, Kiran stumbled upon a well-reputed financial article that predicted a substantial correction in the stock market. Panic gripped him. Fearing the loss of his hard-earned savings, he made a hasty decision. In a rush, he liquidated all his investments and poured everything into bonds, seeking safety and stability.

However, Kiran's timing couldn't have been worse. Just days after he exited the stock market, it embarked on an astonishing bull run. Stocks soared to new highs, and the market seemed unstoppable, gaining a whopping 10% in a single month. Kiran watched helplessly from the sidelines, eagerly awaiting a pullback. But the market had other plans—it continued to set new records week after week.

As the market's valuations climbed to seemingly unsustainable levels, Kiran remained cautious. He believed that a correction was imminent, despite the relentless upward trend. He stayed invested in bonds for an extended period, frustrated that he had missed out on the unprecedented bull run.

Kiran's internal struggle continued. He kicked himself for putting so much trust in a single article, realizing that it might have been created to generate hype and views for the media. Slowly, he began to regain confidence in the stock market. He returned to his familiar strategy of selling covered calls, combining the lessons he had learned with the discipline he had honed over the years.

In the end, Kiran found peace with his investment journey. He realized that even though he had missed out on a remarkable bull run, he had made the best decisions he could at the time with the information available. With a renewed sense of confidence and a commitment to his strategy, Kiran continued to navigate the ever-changing waters of the stock market, embracing both the highs and lows of his trading adventure.

Trader Story 3: "Navigating the Tempest of Market Predictions"

Enter Ganesh, an investor who had dedicated his life savings to the stock market. His strategy was built on the foundation of selling out-of-the-money (OTM) call options, which had been profitable for him. However, his journey took a tumultuous turn during the outbreak of the COVID-19 pandemic.

As the world grappled with uncertainty, the stock market exhibited wild fluctuations. Ganesh couldn't escape the barrage of sensational news and the constant chatter on social forums. Panic seemed to be spreading as rapidly as the virus itself. The stock market, which had been comfortably trading at 12,000, suddenly plummeted by 2%.

Amid the chaos, Ganesh stumbled upon a research report authored by a well-known analyst. This report predicted a catastrophic market correction, one that would send the market plunging to 3,000—a staggering 75% decline.

As days passed and the market continued its descent, Ganesh found himself placing more trust in the analyst's prediction. With each dip, he became increasingly convinced that the market was destined for a crash. When the market touched 10,000, Ganesh decided he couldn't ignore the analyst's wisdom any longer. He made the fateful decision to liquidate his entire portfolio, believing that he could buy back in at the predicted bottom of 3,000.

However, fate had other plans. In just a few short months, the market, much to Ganesh's frustration, embarked on an astonishing recovery. It soared to 15,000, leaving him bewildered and regretful.

Ganesh's experience served as a harsh lesson. He realized that predictions of market crashes and booms were a dime a dozen. Analysts often claimed to have foreseen major market movements, but in reality, these predictions were often nothing more than random guesses, conveniently justified after the fact.

Regaining his composure, Ganesh returned to the market with a newfound perspective. He recognized that while external influences and predictions could be tempting, the market's true nature was often unpredictable. Ganesh resumed his investments with caution, knowing that his reactions to external influences had cost him dearly. His journey through the tempest of market predictions had ultimately taught him the importance of resilience and disciplined decision-making in the world of trading.

13. Options Trading and Life Balance: Avoiding Burnout and Stress

Life balance in options trading refers to the equilibrium between one's trading activities and the various facets of their personal life. It entails maintaining harmony between the pursuit of trading success and the need for physical, emotional, and social well-being.

Achieving and sustaining life balance is paramount for long-term trading success. The demanding and often high-stress nature of options trading can take a toll on traders' health and relationships if not managed effectively. This chapter explores strategies and practices to help traders strike that crucial balance, ensuring their trading journey is both financially rewarding and personally fulfilling.

The High-Stress Nature of Options Trading

Options trading is renowned for its inherently high-stress environment, characterized by various stressors that traders face on a daily basis. Understanding these stressors is crucial for anyone embarking on an options trading journey:

Market Volatility: Options, particularly those with shorter expiration periods, are highly sensitive to market fluctuations. Rapid price movements can trigger anxiety and stress, as traders must make quick decisions to mitigate potential losses.

Risk Exposure: Options inherently involve risk, as traders can lose their entire investment if the market doesn't move as anticipated. This constant exposure to financial risk can lead to chronic stress.

Uncertainty: The financial markets are unpredictable, and unexpected events can impact option prices. Traders often find themselves navigating through a sea of uncertainty, adding to their stress levels.

Pressure to Perform: Options traders often feel immense pressure to consistently profit, as well as to outperform benchmarks and competitors. This pressure can lead to performance anxiety and stress.

Information Overload: Traders need to process vast amounts of information, including market news, technical indicators, and economic data. Information overload can lead to decision fatigue and mental exhaustion.

Long Trading Hours: Options markets operate at various hours, depending on the asset and exchange. This extended trading day can disrupt traders' work-life balance and contribute to stress.

Financial Pressure: Many options traders use significant capital, and the pressure to generate returns can be overwhelming. Losses not only affect traders' portfolios but can also have broader financial consequences.

Complexity: Options trading strategies can be intricate and require a deep understanding of financial markets. The complexity of these strategies can be mentally taxing and contribute to stress

Lack of Control: The financial markets are influenced by various external factors, including geopolitical events and economic data releases. Traders often feel a lack of control over these events, leading to stress.

Sleep Disruption: Monitoring the markets around the clock can disrupt sleep patterns, leading to sleep deprivation. Sleep-deprived traders may experience reduced cognitive function and heightened stress levels.

Isolation: Options trading can be a solitary endeavor, especially for retail traders. The isolation and lack of social interaction can contribute to feelings of loneliness and stress.

Overtrading: The desire to maximize profits can lead to overtrading, where traders take excessive risks or execute too many trades. Overtrading can result in significant stress and financial losses.

Technology Failures: Reliance on technology is integral to options trading. Technical glitches, platform outages, or slow internet connections can be extremely stressful, particularly during critical trading moments.

These stressors collectively create a high-pressure environment in options trading. Traders who are aware of these challenges and develop effective coping strategies are better equipped to manage stress and maintain their mental and emotional well-being while pursuing success in the options market.

Recognizing Burnout and Chronic Stress

Burnout and chronic stress can have severe consequences on a trader's well-being and performance. Understanding the signs and symptoms is crucial for timely intervention and prevention. Here's an in-depth look at how to recognize burnout and chronic stress among options traders:

Signs and Symptoms of Burnout and Chronic Stress:

Emotional Exhaustion: Traders experiencing burnout often feel emotionally drained. They may become easily irritable, cynical, and detached from their work, colleagues, or trading activities.

Physical Symptoms: Chronic stress can manifest physically. Traders may experience headaches, muscle tension, digestive issues, and changes in appetite or sleep patterns.

Reduced Performance: Chronic stress and burnout can impair cognitive functions such as decision-making, problem-solving, and memory. Traders may struggle to concentrate and make mistakes in their trading strategies.

Loss of Motivation: Burnout can lead to a loss of enthusiasm and motivation for trading. Traders may no longer find enjoyment or purpose in their work, and their commitment wanes.

Increased Anxiety: Chronic stress often accompanies heightened anxiety. Traders may worry excessively about their trades, financial outcomes, or the future, leading to restlessness and apprehension.

Withdrawal: Burnout can prompt traders to withdraw from social interactions and trading-related activities. They may isolate themselves from colleagues, friends, and trading communities.

Insomnia: Chronic stress can disrupt sleep patterns, leading to insomnia. Traders may struggle to fall asleep or stay asleep, further exacerbating their stress levels.

Neglect of Self-Care: Burnout may cause traders to neglect self-care routines, such as exercise, a balanced diet, and relaxation. This can lead to physical and emotional deterioration.

Increased Substance Use: Some traders turn to alcohol, drugs, or other substances as a coping mechanism for stress, which can further worsen their well-being.

Loss of Confidence: Chronic stress and burnout can erode a trader's confidence in their abilities. They may doubt their skills, strategies, and judgment.

The Impact of Stress on Trading Performance and Personal Life

Stress is a pervasive force that can permeate both a trader's performance and their personal life, often with detrimental effects.

Impact on Trading Performance:

Impaired Decision-Making: Stress has a profound impact on decision-making in the trading world. It can lead to emotional trading, where traders make impulsive decisions driven by fear or greed. This emotional decision-making can result in erratic trading behavior and substantial losses.

Loss Aversion: Stress often heightens the fear of losing money. Traders, under stress, may become excessively risk-averse, leading them to exit trades prematurely or avoid taking calculated risks. This can result in missed profit opportunities.

Risk Management Challenges: Stress disrupts effective risk management. Traders may experience fluctuations in their risk tolerance, becoming excessively risk-averse during stressful periods or overly aggressive when trying to recover losses. This inconsistency in risk management can lead to substantial losses.

Eroding Trading Discipline: Discipline is crucial for trading success, but stress can undermine it. Traders under stress may engage in overtrading, making excessive trades outside their strategy in the hopes of recouping losses. They may also abandon their trading plans for impulsive decisions.

Impact on Personal Life and Relationships:

Strained Relationships: Chronic stress from trading can strain personal relationships with family, friends, and significant others. Traders may become irritable, distant, or preoccupied with their trading, neglecting personal connections.

Health Issues: Prolonged stress can lead to various health problems, including high blood pressure, anxiety disorders, and depression. These health issues can further exacerbate stress and hinder overall well-being.

Reduced Quality of Life: The constant pressure and anxiety associated with trading-related stress can diminish one's overall quality of life. Enjoyment, relaxation, and leisure activities may take a backseat to trading concerns.

Strategies for Stress Management in Options Trading:
Options trading can be highly stressful, but with effective stress management strategies, traders can maintain their emotional well-being while making sound decisions. Here are practical tips for managing stress in options trading:

1. Risk Management:

Set Risk Limits: Establish predefined risk limits for each trade and adhere to them. This helps reduce the anxiety of potential large losses and keeps trading within your comfort zone.

Position Sizing: Determine the appropriate position size based on your risk tolerance and account size. Avoid overleveraging, which can lead to excessive stress during market fluctuations.

2. Trading Plan:

Create a Solid Plan: Develop a comprehensive trading plan that includes entry and exit strategies, risk management rules, and criteria for selecting trades. Having a plan reduces impulsive decision-making under stress.

Stick to Your Plan: Discipline is key. Consistently following your trading plan, even during stressful moments, helps maintain a sense of control and confidence.

3. Mindfulness and Self-Awareness:

Stay Present: Practice mindfulness techniques like deep breathing or meditation to stay focused on the current moment, rather than worrying about past losses or future uncertainties.

Emotional Awareness: Recognize your emotions while trading. Take breaks or step back if you notice overwhelming stress or fear influencing your decisions.

4. Continuous Learning:

Stay Informed: Keep yourself updated on market news and economic events that may impact your trades. Knowledge can reduce uncertainty and anxiety.

Educational Resources: Invest time in learning about options trading strategies and psychology. The more you understand, the more confident you'll feel.

5. Support Network:

Seek Guidance: If you're struggling with stress, consider consulting a therapist or trading psychologist. They can provide valuable coping strategies and emotional support.

Talk to Peers: Connect with other traders or join trading communities to share experiences and insights. Peer support can be immensely helpful in stressful times.

6. Physical Well-Being:

Exercise Regularly: Engage in physical activities like jogging, yoga, or gym workouts. Exercise releases endorphins, reducing stress and promoting overall well-being.

Balanced Diet: Maintain a healthy diet rich in nutrients. Avoid excessive caffeine and sugar, as they can lead to energy crashes and increased stress.

7. Breaks and Rest:

Scheduled Breaks: Take short breaks during trading hours to relax and clear your mind. Avoid staring at the screen for extended periods.

Sufficient Sleep: Prioritize adequate and consistent sleep. Lack of sleep can exacerbate stress and negatively impact decision-making.

8. Disconnect:

Digital Detox: Occasionally disconnect from screens and trading-related news to prevent information overload. Give yourself time to unwind and recharge.

9. Acceptance and Perspective:

Accept Losses: Understand that losses are part of trading. Embrace them as opportunities for learning and growth rather than failures.

Long-Term View: Keep the bigger picture in mind. Single trades should be seen as part of a larger trading strategy and not overly fixated upon.

Maintaining a Good Trading-Personal Life Balance:

Balancing options trading with personal life is essential for mental and emotional well-being. Here are practical tips for achieving this balance:

1. Set Boundaries:

Designate Trading Hours: Define specific hours for trading and stick to them. This prevents overtrading and allows time for personal life.

Create a Trading Routine: Establish a daily routine that includes time for family, hobbies, and relaxation.

2. Time Management:

Plan Ahead: Allocate time for trading and personal activities on a daily and weekly basis. Efficient time management reduces stress and maintains balance.

Prioritize Personal Time: Recognize the importance of personal life and allocate time accordingly. Avoid letting trading consume your entire day.

3. Family and Communication:

Involve Your Family: Educate your family about your trading activities and their potential impact. Open communication fosters understanding and support.

Quality Time: Dedicate quality time to your family and loved ones. Be fully present when you're with them to nurture your personal relationships.

4. Hobbies and Interests:

Pursue Hobbies: Make time for activities you enjoy outside of trading. Hobbies provide a healthy outlet for stress and contribute to life satisfaction.

Maintain Interests: Stay engaged in interests and passions that make you feel fulfilled.

5. Self-Care:

Personal Well-Being: Prioritize self-care. This includes physical health, mental well-being, and relaxation. Take breaks to recharge.

Balancing options trading with personal life requires careful planning and discipline. By implementing these strategies, traders can lead fulfilling lives while successfully navigating the challenges of options trading.

"Many traders initially enter the market with the goal of improving their quality of life, but it's common for them to become consumed by trading and lose sight of their original intentions."

Stress: Trader Case Studies
Trader Story 2: Reckless Trade to Humble Life

Rajesh had achieved remarkable success as an options trader. He had diligently grown his trading account and was consistently earning profits. He had dedicated himself to mastering the intricacies of options trading, from understanding various strategies to diving deep into technical analysis. But as his passion for trading grew, so did his obsession with it.

His relentless focus on the market came at a cost. Rajesh found himself checking his mobile for news updates even during dinner dates with his girlfriend. He couldn't resist the urge to make trades, even if it meant interrupting precious moments with his loved one. This constant stress and irritability took a toll on his personal life.

Frequent fights with his girlfriend became the norm, highlighting Rajesh's lack of emotional intelligence. Unable to strike a balance between his passion for trading and nurturing his relationship, he unknowingly pushed his girlfriend away. One day, she decided to move on and found someone else.

Devastated by the breakup and the loss of his love, Rajesh's world crumbled. In a moment of frustration and stress, he made a reckless decision. He threw all his money into out-of-the-money options on an expiry day, hoping for a miracle that would either make him an instant millionaire or leave him with nothing.

The market, however, had its own plans, which seldom aligned with his wishes. Rajesh's options ended up expiring worthless, resulting in a staggering 90% loss of his trading account. Now in debt, with only an average-paying job, Rajesh found himself at the lowest point in his life.

But Rajesh was not one to stay down for long. He embarked on a challenging journey to rebuild his life. It took five long years of hard work, discipline, and resilience to climb his way back to where he was before the ill-fated trade. Along the way, he learned valuable lessons about managing stress and the importance of work-life balance.

Eventually, Rajesh found love again and married someone who understood and supported his passions while helping him maintain a healthy balance. This trader's story serves as a powerful reminder that success in trading is not just about financial gains; it's also about mastering the art of managing stress and preserving the other precious aspects of life.

Trader Story 2: Finding Wealth in Life's Balance

Ankit, a finance professional with a burning desire to become a millionaire, was determined to chase his dreams relentlessly. He had secured a night shift job intentionally, with a plan to work all night and trade during the day, aiming to create two streams of income.

For months, he clung to this grueling routine, surviving on minimal sleep and a diet that could hardly sustain his energy. His weekends were consumed by market analyses and learning, leaving no room for personal time or enjoyment. Ankit's world became a relentless pursuit of money, and he lost sight of everything else.

As the days turned into nights and back into days, Ankit's lack of sleep and inadequate nutrition began to take its toll. The constant stress of juggling two demanding schedules pushed him to the brink. He isolated himself, working from home and trading obsessively, leaving his health in a deteriorating state.

One fateful day, it all came crashing down. Ankit collapsed, unconscious and frail. Rushed to the hospital, he received a sobering diagnosis from the doctor—sleep deprivation and malnutrition had taken a severe toll on his health. The doctor's stern warning echoed in his ears; if he continued on this path, the consequences could be irreversible.

Ankit faced a moment of reckoning. He realized that he had been so focused on accumulating wealth that he had neglected the most valuable asset of all—his health. The wake-up call was harsh, but it was also a turning point.

Determined to regain control of his life, Ankit embarked on a journey of recovery. He bid farewell to his night shift job, embracing a regular daytime position. He scaled back his trading hours significantly, prioritizing quality over quantity. Most importantly, he made time for self-care, incorporating exercise into his daily routine and rediscovering his love for music as a hobby.

In his own words, Ankit reflected on his transformation: "I've never truly lived my life until now." He discovered that wealth wasn't just about money; it was about finding balance, nurturing his well-being, and cherishing the simple joys of life. Ankit's story serves as a powerful reminder that true prosperity lies in harmonizing financial success with a rich and fulfilling life.

Trader Story 3: Saravanan's Stressful Gamble

Saravanan was a trader with a dream. He had started small, steadily growing his trading account month by month, earning a reasonable return on his investments. He had a comfortable job, but the lure of making it big in the trading world was irresistible.

One day, an idea crossed Saravanan's mind that would change his life, but not necessarily for the better. He decided to take a huge risk by borrowing a substantial amount as a personal loan and depositing it into his trading account. His rationale was simple: if he could just generate returns equivalent to the loan's EMI, he would be left with a significant profit in a few years.

This decision put immense pressure on Saravanan. Suddenly, he was no longer trading for leisure or gradual growth but was chasing a specific monthly income target. The burden of this self-imposed deadline started to weigh heavily on him.

The first month under this new pressure was a disappointment. Saravanan couldn't achieve the returns he needed even to cover the interest component of the loan. The second month wasn't any better; he ended with a small loss. Stress began to consume him as he saw his dream of financial success slipping away.

Determined to make everything right, Saravanan entered the third month with a sense of desperation. In an attempt to catch up and meet his monthly target, he increased the size of his trades and took on more risk than ever before. Unfortunately, this risky approach led to massive losses, leaving his trading account in shambles.

It was a painful wake-up call for Saravanan. He realized that trading was not a guaranteed path to regular income. The market didn't adhere to his personal financial timetable. It was a harsh lesson, but it prompted him to reflect on his choices.

Saravanan decided to take responsibility for his financial decisions. He began repaying the personal loan's EMI from his regular salary, avoiding the dangerous practice of using borrowed funds for trading. Recognizing the need to rebuild his mindset, he took a year-long trading break to clear his mind and develop a more disciplined and rational approach to trading.

Saravanan's story serves as a stark reminder of the dangers of trading under immense stress and unrealistic expectations. It highlights the importance of responsible risk management and the need to approach trading as a long-term journey rather than a shortcut to quick riches. Saravanan learned the hard way that trading should never be rushed, and patience and prudence are essential attributes for success in the financial markets.

14: Trading Psychology in Different Market Conditions: Bull, Bear, and Sideways

Introduction to Market Conditions

Market conditions refer to the prevailing state of financial markets, which can be broadly categorized into three primary phases: bull markets, bear markets, and sideways or range-bound markets. Each of these conditions presents a unique set of challenges and opportunities for options traders.

Bull Markets: A bull market is characterized by rising asset prices, investor optimism, and an overall positive sentiment. In such conditions, traders often encounter opportunities for buying call options or employing strategies that capitalize on upward price movements. The significance of recognizing a bull market lies in seizing opportunities for growth and expansion while managing the accompanying euphoria and complacency.

Bear Markets: A bear market, in contrast, signifies declining asset prices, increased pessimism, and a prevailing negative sentiment. Traders in a bear market may focus on strategies such as buying put options or employing bearish spreads. Understanding bear markets is vital for protecting capital, managing risk, and potentially profiting from falling prices, all while dealing with fear and uncertainty.

Sideways or Range-Bound Markets: Sideways or range-bound markets are characterized by asset prices that move within a relatively narrow trading range. In such conditions, traders often employ strategies like iron condors or butterflies that capitalize on low volatility and price stability. Recognizing range-bound markets is important for generating income through options premiums, but traders must remain patient and vigilant for potential breakouts.

To thrive in the diverse landscape of options trading, traders must adapt their psychology to suit the specific challenges and opportunities presented by different market conditions. Here's how:

Flexibility: Traders need to cultivate flexibility and the ability to shift between different strategies and mindsets as market conditions evolve. Being overly attached to a single approach can limit adaptability.

Emotional Resilience: Developing emotional resilience is essential, as different market conditions can evoke distinct emotions. In bull markets, overconfidence can be a pitfall, while bear markets may induce fear and panic. Emotional awareness and self-regulation are key.

Risk Management: Effective risk management becomes even more critical in volatile or uncertain markets. Traders must be prepared to adjust their position sizes, employ protective measures, and adapt their risk tolerance accordingly.

Continuous Learning: Markets are dynamic, and successful traders never stop learning. Adapting to changing market conditions requires staying updated with market news, learning new strategies, and refining existing ones.

Mental Discipline: Traders should maintain mental discipline, avoiding impulsive decisions driven by emotions. A well-defined trading plan can serve as a guiding framework.

Patience and Timing: Recognizing market conditions and patiently waiting for the right opportunities are key components of thriving in various markets. Traders must know when to act and when to stay on the sidelines.

Trading Psychology in a Bull Market

Bull markets are times of optimism, rising asset prices, and widespread positivity in the financial markets. While they offer opportunities for profit, they also present unique psychological challenges for options traders.

Psychological Challenges and Opportunities in a Bull Market:

Overconfidence: One of the primary psychological challenges during a bull market is overconfidence. As asset prices consistently rise, traders may begin to believe that their strategies are infallible. This overconfidence can lead to excessive risk-taking, neglecting risk management, and complacency.

Fear of Missing Out (FOMO): Bull markets often induce FOMO in traders. The fear of missing out on lucrative gains can push traders to enter positions hastily without proper analysis. FOMO-driven decisions may lead to impulsive actions and losses.

Regret Aversion: Traders in a bull market may develop regret aversion. They fear missing out on potential gains, and this fear can keep them from making rational decisions to exit positions when necessary. This can lead to holding onto trades longer than advisable and increased risk exposure.

Confirmation Bias: Bull markets can reinforce confirmation bias, where traders seek information that confirms their bullish outlook while ignoring or downplaying contrary indicators. This bias can prevent traders from seeing potential warning signs.

Emotional Attachment: Traders may become emotionally attached to positions that have been successful during a bull run. Letting go of these positions can be challenging, even when it's clear that profit-taking is prudent.

Strategies for Maintaining Discipline and Managing Risk in a Bull Market:

Stick to Your Trading Plan: Traders should have a well-defined trading plan in place that includes entry and exit strategies, risk management rules, and profit-taking targets. Adhering to this plan is crucial to avoid impulsive decisions.

Set Realistic Goals: While bull markets offer opportunities for profit, traders should set realistic profit targets. Greed can lead to overtrading, so it's essential to be content with reasonable gains.

Stay Informed: Continuously educate yourself about the market. Staying informed about economic indicators, corporate earnings reports, and broader market trends can help you make informed decisions.

Use Stop-Loss Orders: Implement stop-loss orders to limit potential losses. This is a vital tool for risk management, especially when emotions run high.

Maintain Emotional Control: Recognize the emotional impact of a bull market and strive to maintain emotional control. Avoid making decisions based on euphoria or fear.

Regularly Review and Reassess: Periodically review your positions and reassess your strategies. Be willing to adjust your approach if market conditions change.

Trading Psychology in a Bear Market

A bear market, characterized by falling asset prices, pessimism, and widespread fear, presents distinctive psychological challenges for options traders.

Psychological Challenges in a Bear Market:

Fear and Panic: Fear is a dominant emotion in a bear market. As asset prices plummet, traders often experience panic and anxiety, which can lead to impulsive decisions such as selling assets at steep losses or exiting the market altogether.

Loss Aversion: Loss aversion, a common cognitive bias, is amplified in a bear market. Traders become more averse to realizing losses and may hold onto losing positions, hoping for a rebound. This can lead to further losses and heightened emotional distress.

Recency Bias: Traders may exhibit recency bias by placing excessive weight on recent negative market events, assuming that these trends will persist indefinitely. This bias can lead to a lack of adaptability and an inability to see potential opportunities for profit.

Herd Mentality: A bear market often triggers herd mentality, where traders follow the actions of the majority. This can result in crowded trades and exaggerated market movements, making it challenging to make rational decisions.

Strategies for Emotional Resilience and Risk Management in a Bear Market:

Risk Management is Paramount: In a bear market, risk management takes center stage. Implement strict stop-loss orders and position sizing strategies to limit potential losses.

Stay Informed but Avoid Overexposure: While it's essential to stay informed about market developments, avoid overexposure to negative news. Excessive consumption of pessimistic information can amplify fear and anxiety.

Preparedness is Key: Have a well-defined trading plan that includes both entry and exit strategies. Being prepared for various scenarios can help mitigate impulsive reactions.

Mindful Trading: Practicing mindfulness can help traders remain calm and make rational decisions. Techniques such as deep breathing and meditation can reduce stress and anxiety.

Long-Term Perspective: Remember that bear markets are temporary. Taking a long-term perspective can help you endure short-term losses with the confidence that markets eventually recover.

Consult with a Mentor or Advisor: Seek guidance from experienced traders or financial advisors during bear markets. Their insights and perspective can be invaluable.

Trading Psychology in a Sideways Market

A sideways or range-bound market, characterized by limited price movement and uncertainty about the direction of assets, demands a unique psychological approach from traders.

Psychological Dynamics in a Sideways Market:

Patience and Frustration: Sideways markets often test a trader's patience. The lack of clear trends and repetitive price fluctuations can lead to frustration and impulsive decision-making.

Uncertainty: Traders in a sideways market must contend with heightened uncertainty. Predicting short-term price movements becomes more challenging, making it harder to execute trades with confidence.

Overtrading: Some traders may succumb to the temptation of overtrading in a sideways market, making frequent trades to compensate for the lack of significant price movement. This can result in excessive transaction costs and losses.

Stress from Ambiguity: The ambiguity of a sideways market can generate stress, as traders grapple with uncertainty about when or if a breakout or trend reversal will occur.

Strategies for Trading in a Sideways Market:

Exercise Patience: Recognize that patience is paramount in a sideways market. Avoid the urge to overtrade or make impulsive decisions. Wait for clear signals and avoid chasing minor price fluctuations.

Range Trading: Consider employing range trading strategies, such as buying near support levels and selling near resistance levels or deploying an iron condor strategy. This approach capitalizes on price oscillations within a defined range.

Stay Informed: Keep yourself informed about major economic events or news that could potentially break the market out of its sideways pattern. Be prepared to adapt your strategy accordingly.

Use Technical Analysis: Utilize technical analysis tools such as Bollinger Bands or moving averages to identify potential breakout points or changes in market sentiment.

Adapting Trading Strategies to Market Conditions

The ability to adapt trading strategies to match prevailing market conditions is a hallmark of successful traders. Market conditions are dynamic and can vary widely, including bull markets, bear markets, and sideways or range-bound markets. Here's why adapting trading strategies is essential:

Maximizing Profit Potential: Different market conditions offer distinct profit opportunities. Adapting allows traders to leverage strategies that are most likely to succeed in the current environment, thus maximizing profit potential.

Risk Management: Effective adaptation also involves managing risk. Traders can adjust their positions and strategies to mitigate risk exposure when market conditions become more uncertain or volatile.

Capital Preservation: Preserving trading capital is paramount. Adapting strategies ensures that capital is not unnecessarily exposed to unfavorable market conditions, helping traders maintain their longevity in the market.

Options Strategies and Market Environments:

Options traders have a versatile toolkit of strategies, each suited to specific market conditions. Here's how different options strategies align with various market environments:

Bull Markets:

In a bullish market, options traders often employ strategies like covered calls, where they hold a long position in the underlying asset while selling call options to generate income.

Bull put spreads and naked puts are also popular, allowing traders to benefit from the upward trend while managing risk.

Bear Markets:

In bearish markets, traders may use bear call spreads, which involve selling a call option with a higher strike price and buying one with a lower strike, to profit from falling prices.

Long puts provide a straightforward way to profit from bearish trends, as the value of the put option increases as the underlying asset's price decreases.

Sideways Markets:

In range-bound or sideways markets, options traders can employ iron condors, where they simultaneously sell both a call spread and a put spread with strike prices outside the expected trading range.

Calendar spreads can also be effective, as they benefit from low volatility and time decay while potentially profiting from small price movements.

Market Condition: Trader Case Studies

Trader Story 1: Kumar's Costly Panic

Kumar was an investor with a strong belief in the power of long-term holdings. He had accumulated a significant portfolio of stocks over the years while also dabbling in part-time options trading to supplement his income. Life was good, and his investments were growing steadily.

Then, the unexpected happened. The COVID-19 pandemic struck, sending shockwaves through global markets. Fear and uncertainty were palpable as stock prices plummeted, and market sentiment turned pessimistic. Kumar watched in dismay as the market took a nosedive, with indices shedding nearly 50% of their value.

Fear gripped Kumar like never before. Panic set in, and he couldn't bear to see the value of his long-term investments dwindling rapidly. In a moment of desperation, he made a fateful decision – he sold all of his investments, cutting his losses at the worst possible time.

However, Kumar believed he could recover some of his losses through options trading. He bought put options, anticipating that the market would continue to plummet. The volatility index, or VIX, was hovering around a staggering 80, indicating extreme market turbulence.

But Kumar was so consumed by panic and the losses in his long-term portfolio that he failed to realize a crucial detail. The panic had sent options premiums skyrocketing, making them incredibly expensive. He had entered the options market when prices were at their peak.

As the market continued its downward spiral, Kumar's prediction appeared to be coming true. However, there was a cruel twist of fate awaiting him. The extreme volatility that had initially driven up options prices now began to subside, causing premiums to crash. Kumar's options positions lost value rapidly, and he watched helplessly as his account balance dwindled.

In the end, Kumar had almost wiped out his entire trading account, which he had carefully built over multiple years. His panic-driven decisions had cost him dearly. He realized that reacting out of fear and making impulsive decisions in the financial markets could lead to disastrous consequences.

Kumar's story serves as a sobering lesson on the importance of maintaining composure during times of market turmoil. It underscores the significance of having a well-thought-out trading strategy and the perils of allowing emotions to dictate financial decisions. Kumar learned that in the world of trading, emotions can be a trader's worst enemy, and a rational, disciplined approach is essential for long-term success.

Trader Story 2: Martingale Misadventure

Rakesh was a casual options trader who had seen his fair share of market ups and downs. During a particularly robust bull run, he found himself inundated with articles, news reports, and technical analyses all pointing to a glaring truth – the stock markets were scaling unprecedented heights, and many believed they were overvalued.

As days turned into weeks and the markets continued their relentless ascent, Rakesh remained a passive observer. He watched as prices climbed higher and higher, seemingly defying gravity. However, he couldn't resist the temptation to participate in the action.

One day, Rakesh made a calculated move. He decided to dip his toes into the bullish frenzy by selling some at-the-money call options. It seemed like a reasonable strategy, given the market's euphoria. His initial foray, though, resulted in a small loss, but Rakesh remained undeterred.

In fact, Rakesh was oddly delighted. He saw the prices soar even higher, and his first loss appeared trivial in comparison. A thought began to take root in his mind – what if he increased the position size? After all, the market was bound to correct at some point, right? It was a classic case of the gambler's fallacy, where one assumes that future outcomes are influenced by past events, even in situations where each event is independent.

Emboldened by this line of thinking, Rakesh doubled his position, selling more at-the-money call options. He was convinced that sooner or later, the market would have to come down, and when it did, he would recoup all his previous losses. Statistically, it seemed like a winning strategy. The chances of incurring a loss multiple times in a row were less than 5%, according to Rakesh's calculations.

But the markets cared little for Rakesh's calculations or convictions. Instead of reversing, they defied logic and continued their ascent, churning out more losses for him. Unfazed by the mounting financial setbacks, Rakesh was resolute. He quadrupled his next trade, believing that this time the market had to relent.

Again, he was met with disappointment as the market surged even higher. Determined to stick with his chosen path, Rakesh convinced himself that the market's behavior was irrational and unsustainable. He made an audacious move, octupling his position size, selling even more at-the-money call options. It was a high-stakes gamble, a bet that the market simply couldn't continue its relentless climb indefinitely.

But markets, as they often do, proved Rakesh wrong. Instead of reversing, they maintained their upward trajectory, leaving Rakesh with staggering losses that wiped out most of his trading account. He was left in a precarious financial and emotional state, grappling with the harsh reality that markets can remain irrational far longer than one's account can remain solvent.

Rakesh's story serves as a cautionary tale about the dangers of the martingale method and the fallacy of assuming that markets will correct themselves on one's timeline. It illustrates how emotions, unchecked by discipline and risk management, can lead to financial ruin. In the end, Rakesh learned the hard way that trading should never resemble a gamble, and careful planning and prudent risk management are paramount in navigating the markets.

Trader Story 3: Straddle Stumble and Rebound

Ganesh, an experienced options trader, had built his trading success on the foundation of the short straddle strategy. This strategy involved simultaneously selling both a call option and a put option with the same strike price and expiration date, betting on the stability and limited price movement of the underlying asset.

For a significant period, this approach had rewarded Ganesh with consistent profits. However, as every seasoned trader knows, the markets can be unpredictable, and unexpected turbulence can disrupt even the most reliable strategies.

One month, Ganesh found himself facing precisely this situation. The market took an unexpected nosedive, inducing panic and significantly increasing market volatility as measured by the VIX. These abrupt changes in market conditions presented Ganesh with unfamiliar challenges.

The market downturn not only impacted his short straddle positions but also altered the delta of his trades. This unexpected change exacerbated his losses, sending him into uncharted territory.

Ganesh was not one to back down easily. He believed that the increased losses driven by the spike in VIX were transitory and would eventually subside. To counter the altered delta risk, he opted to sell additional call options, a move he deemed sensible to mitigate his mounting losses. However, the market had more surprises in store.

The continued market decline drove Ganesh's put options deep into the money, resulting in substantial losses despite his sold call options. His efforts to contain the damage by selling even more call options only deepened his dilemma. He soon reached the limit of his margin.

Ganesh was at a crossroads, facing a pivotal decision. Should he cut his losses, salvaging what remained of his account, or should he hold on, convinced that the market would eventually reverse in his favor? The month had proven to be exceptionally challenging, erasing several months' worth of hard-earned profits.

However, Ganesh was not one to admit defeat easily. He meticulously recorded every trade and subjected his strategies to thorough analysis. Recognizing the necessity for change, he set out to adapt his trading approach to the new market conditions.

After exhaustive analysis and reflection, Ganesh modified his short straddle strategy. He introduced elements that would allow it to withstand not only stable market conditions but also the unexpected twists and turns of volatile markets. He embraced the value of flexibility and diversification in his trading.

Ganesh's story serves as a powerful reminder of the need for traders, regardless of their experience, to continually refine and adapt their strategies. The markets are ever-evolving, and even the most successful traders must be prepared to adjust when faced with unexpected challenges. Through resilience and adaptability, Ganesh emerged from this experience stronger and better equipped to navigate the complexities of options trading.

15: Creating Your Personal Trading Psychology Plan: A Step-by-Step Guide

A personalized trading psychology plan is your invaluable tool for navigating the complexities of trading. Think of it as your strategic compass, guiding you through the unpredictable terrain of financial markets. This plan plays a pivotal role in bolstering your trading discipline and sharpening your decision-making skills. Just as a seasoned hiker relies on a well-thought-out plan to conquer challenging trails, traders can rely on their psychology plan to conquer the emotional ups and downs of the trading journey. In this chapter, we'll delve into why this plan is crucial and how it can empower traders to stay focused, make sound judgments, and thrive in the dynamic world of trading.

Self-Assessment and Goal Setting
Evaluating Your Current Trading Mindset and Emotional Tendencies

Before diving into the markets, it's crucial to recognize your existing trading mindset and emotional tendencies. Below are some questions you can ask yourself and write down an honest and detailed answer to assess yourself.

What is your emotional responses to gains and losses?

The question of your emotional responses to gains and losses in trading is a fundamental self-assessment that can significantly impact your trading psychology. Here are possible answers and their interpretations:

Euphoria on Gains and Devastation on Losses: If you find yourself feeling euphoric when you make profits and devastated when you incur losses, it suggests that your emotional responses are highly reactive. While experiencing positive emotions on gains is natural, extreme euphoria can lead to overconfidence and risky decisions. Conversely, extreme devastation on losses can lead to impulsive actions, such as revenge trading or excessive risk-taking. In any of these cases reducing position size to minimize the emotional response is highly recommended

Indifference or Minimized Reaction: Some traders may report that they react with indifference or minimal emotional response to both gains and losses. While this may appear ideal, it's essential to ensure that this response is not due to emotional detachment, which can lead to complacency. A balanced response that acknowledges gains and losses without being emotionally overwhelmed or detached is ideal.

Overconfidence on Gains and Denial on Losses: If you tend to become overconfident when you make profits and deny or downplay losses, it indicates a psychological bias known as the "overconfidence bias." Overconfidence can lead to neglecting risk management, increasing position sizes excessively, and ultimately incurring significant losses due to complacency. This is very similar to the first one, reduce position sizing immediately to arrive at ideal emotional state.

Fear on Gains and Paralysis on Losses: Some traders may experience fear or anxiety when they make gains, fearing that they might lose them. On the flip side, they might become paralyzed or unable to make decisions when faced with losses. This emotional response can hinder effective decision-making and lead to missed opportunities or prolonged losing streaks.

Emotional Balance: Achieving emotional balance means experiencing moderate positive emotions on gains and acknowledging losses without being overly devastated. This response is typically associated with traders who have developed emotional resilience and discipline. They are less likely to make impulsive decisions based on emotions.

Changing Emotional Responses: Emotional responses to gains and losses can change over time with experience and self-awareness.

Traders may evolve from initially experiencing extreme emotions to developing a more balanced response as they gain experience and learn to manage their emotions better. However, changing emotional responses every trade is not ideal and indicates inconsistent risk management system being followed, risking high on some trades and low on some trades are not ideal as in long run the risk to reward will hamper trading performance, preparing a consistent risk management and position sizing is ideal.

What is your risk tolerance?

When assessing your risk tolerance as a trader, it's crucial to consider several factors that can influence your ability and willingness to handle risk. Here are possible answers and their interpretations:

High Risk Tolerance: If you believe you have a high risk tolerance, it means you are comfortable with the idea of taking significant risks in pursuit of potentially high returns. You might be more inclined to trade in volatile markets, use leverage, or engage in speculative strategies. However, it's essential to ensure that your risk management is equally robust to mitigate the potential for substantial losses.

Moderate Risk Tolerance: A moderate risk tolerance suggests that you are willing to take some risks, but you prefer a balanced approach. You aim for a mix of conservative and moderately aggressive investments or trading strategies. This approach seeks to balance the pursuit of returns with a degree of risk management and capital preservation.

Low Risk Tolerance: A low risk tolerance indicates that you are cautious and prioritize the preservation of capital over potential gains. You may prefer less volatile assets, lower-risk strategies, and a more conservative approach. This can be beneficial for capital protection but may result in lower returns.

Changing Risk Tolerance: Some traders may find that their risk tolerance changes over time due to various factors like experience, financial circumstances, or life events. It's essential to regularly reassess your risk tolerance to ensure that your trading strategies align with your current comfort level. However, changing risk tolerance multiple times in a day or week is highly not recommended, if your emotions are affected reduce the risk tolerance.

How good are your ability to stay disciplined?

The question of your ability to stay disciplined in trading is crucial for your long-term success. Here are possible answers and their interpretations:

High Discipline: If you believe that you have a high level of discipline in your trading, it suggests that you can stick to your trading plan and strategies even when faced with emotional or external pressures. High discipline is a positive trait and often leads to consistent and profitable trading.

Moderate Discipline: Some traders may consider themselves moderately disciplined. They follow their trading plan most of the time but may occasionally deviate from it due to emotions or impulsive decisions. This level of discipline is common among traders and can still lead to success if the lapses in discipline are infrequent and minor.

Struggling with Discipline: If you find it challenging to maintain discipline in your trading, it indicates that you often deviate from your trading plan, take impulsive actions, or let emotions drive your decisions. This lack of discipline can result in inconsistent and potentially negative trading outcomes. It is recommended to immediately fix this issue, you can choose a mentor who monitors and reviews your trading account regularly, this creates a sense of responsibility. You can even come up with your own set of ideas to improve your discipline in trading.

Variable Discipline: Some traders may experience varying levels of discipline depending on market conditions or personal factors. They might be disciplined in certain situations but struggle in others. It's essential to identify the specific circumstances or triggers that affect your discipline to work on improving consistency. For example: a trader can be disciplined when his personal relationship with their significant other is good, but he trades impulsively when there are some arguments with their significant other

Improving Discipline: If you acknowledge that your discipline needs improvement but you are actively working on it, this is a positive sign. It shows that you are aware of the issue and are taking steps to address it, such as through journaling, mindfulness, or seeking mentorship.

Overconfident Discipline: In some cases, traders may believe they are highly disciplined when, in reality, they are overconfident and unwilling to admit their lapses in discipline. Overconfidence in one's discipline can lead to ignoring warning signs and failing to make necessary adjustments. This is dangerous because the trader will only realise this when they incur a huge loss

What does your past trading patterns and decision-making behaviors conveys?

The question regarding your past trading patterns and decision-making behaviors is a critical aspect of self-assessment in trading. Here are possible answers and their interpretations:

Consistency and Success: If your past trading patterns and behaviors indicate a consistent and successful track record, it suggests that you have developed effective strategies and decision-making skills. This is a positive sign that your approach is working well, and you may want to continue with similar practices.

Inconsistency with Success: In some cases, traders might have experienced periods of success but with inconsistent patterns. This could mean that while you've had profitable trades, there may also be significant losses or deviations from your plan. It's important to review these inconsistencies to understand what led to both successes and failures.

Consistency with Losses: If your trading history shows a consistent pattern of losses or underperformance, it suggests that your current strategies or decision-making behaviors may not be effective. This should prompt you to reevaluate your approach, identify weaknesses, and consider making significant changes to improve your trading.

Impulsivity: Traders who frequently engage in impulsive decision-making behaviors, such as chasing trades, revenge trading, or neglecting stop-loss orders, may find their past patterns characterized by erratic results. Recognizing impulsivity is crucial, as it can lead to losses and significant emotional stress.

Overtrading: Some traders may identify a pattern of overtrading, where they take excessive positions or trade too frequently. This can lead to increased transaction costs, higher risk exposure, and potential burnout. Acknowledging this pattern is the first step toward addressing it and adopting a more measured trading approach.

Risk Management Issues: If your past trading patterns reveal inadequate risk management practices, such as risking too much capital on a single trade or failing to diversify your portfolio, it indicates a need for improvement in risk management skills. Poor risk management can lead to significant losses and should be addressed promptly.

Learning and Adaptation: Traders who recognize that their past patterns and behaviors have taught them valuable lessons about the market may have a growth mindset. They understand that trading is a continuous learning process and are open to adapting and evolving their strategies based on past experiences.

What are your expectations from your options trading career?

The question about expectations from your options trading career is crucial for setting clear goals and aligning your efforts. Here are possible answers and their interpretations:

Wealth Accumulation: If your primary expectation is to accumulate wealth and achieve financial independence through options trading, it suggests that you have a long-term perspective. You are likely committed to disciplined trading and wealth-building strategies, understanding that it may take time to achieve substantial gains.

Income Generation: Some traders view options trading as a means of generating consistent income. If this is your expectation, you are likely focused on strategies that provide regular cash flow, such as selling covered calls or cash-secured puts. Your emphasis is on managing risk while aiming for consistent returns.

Capital Preservation: If your main goal is to protect and preserve your capital, you prioritize risk management and capital preservation strategies. You may be more conservative in your approach, willing to accept lower returns in exchange for lower risk exposure.

Road to Quick Riches: If your expectation from options trading is to quickly amass substantial wealth or achieve significant financial gains in a short period, you may have a more aggressive approach. However, it's important to recognize that trading for quick riches can involve higher risks and potential for significant losses. Traders with this expectation should be aware of the heightened emotional and psychological challenges associated with seeking rapid wealth through trading. It's advisable to balance the desire for quick gains with a realistic understanding of market dynamics and risk management strategies.

Diversification: Some traders engage in options trading to diversify their investment portfolios. If this is your expectation, you aim to reduce risk by spreading your investments across different asset classes, strategies, or market conditions. Diversification can help mitigate losses during market downturns.

Retirement Planning: If you intend to use options trading as a component of your retirement planning, your focus is on creating a nest egg that can provide for your future needs. You likely have a long-term horizon and prioritize strategies that offer consistent returns and capital preservation.

Passive Income: Traders seeking passive income often aim to build a portfolio that generates cash flow with minimal active management. Your expectation is to set up strategies that require less day-to-day attention, allowing you to enjoy your desired lifestyle while still earning income.

Financial Independence: Achieving financial independence is a common expectation among traders. This involves having enough wealth to support your desired lifestyle without relying on traditional employment. You are motivated to grow your trading capital to reach this level of financial freedom.

Challenging and Rewarding Hobby: For some, options trading is seen as a challenging and rewarding hobby. If this is your expectation, you enjoy the intellectual stimulation and excitement of trading, even if it's not your primary source of income. Your primary goal is personal satisfaction and enjoyment. However, experts suggest to choose a sport or any other hobbies like music where the risk is low. Options trading is highly addictive

Building a Trading Routine

A well-structured trading routine is the backbone of consistency and success in the world of trading. In this section, we'll delve into the significance of a structured routine, helping you establish a clear daily, weekly, and monthly trading schedule that aligns with your trading objectives, while also ensuring you have ample time for research, analysis, and personal life.

Below are some questions you can ask yourself and write down an honest and detailed answer to assess yourself.

What's your daily personal life routine, ignoring trading?

This question delves into the trader's ability to maintain a well-rounded life outside of trading. It's crucial for achieving balance and reducing stress. Here are possible answers and their interpretations:

Balanced Personal Routine: This response indicates that the trader has a structured daily routine that prioritizes personal life. It typically includes time for family, hobbies, exercise, and relaxation. A balanced routine implies a healthy approach to life where trading doesn't dominate every aspect, leading to reduced stress and better decision-making in trading.

Demanding 9 to 5 Job: If a trader's daily routine includes a demanding 9 to 5 job along with trading, it highlights their ability to manage time effectively and balance two significant commitments. However, it can also signify a busy and potentially stressful lifestyle, emphasizing the importance of structured routines to manage both work and trading successfully.

Neglected Personal Life: If the answer suggests that personal life is largely neglected or that there is no defined routine, it may indicate an unhealthy obsession with trading. Neglecting personal relationships, health, or leisure activities can lead to burnout and negatively impact both trading and overall happiness.

Erratic or Chaotic Personal Routine: An unpredictable or chaotic personal routine can reflect a lack of structure and discipline. Such a lifestyle can lead to emotional turmoil and hinder the trader's ability to manage the psychological challenges of trading effectively.

Overemphasis on Trading: Some traders might structure their personal lives around trading, dedicating excessive time to monitoring the markets even during personal activities. This behavior can strain relationships and cause undue stress.

Health and Wellness Focus: A personal routine that emphasizes health and wellness, including regular exercise and a balanced diet, indicates a commitment to physical and mental well-being. A healthy body and mind are better equipped to handle the stressors of trading.

Quality Family Time: Allocating quality time for family and loved ones in the daily personal routine signifies a recognition of the importance of nurturing personal relationships. Strong support systems can provide emotional stability during trading challenges.

Continued Learning and Growth: A daily routine that includes time for personal growth, education, or pursuing hobbies outside of trading indicates a holistic approach to life. Personal development can contribute positively to both trading and overall life satisfaction.

Neglected Self-Care: If self-care, including relaxation and leisure activities, is absent from the daily personal routine, it may lead to stress accumulation. Neglecting self-care can eventually impact trading performance and personal happiness.

What's your existing daily trading routine?
This question is a crucial one for traders to ask themselves, as it plays a pivotal role in assessing their trading routine. Here are some possible answers and their interpretations:

Structured Trading Routine: If your answer involves a well-structured daily routine that outlines specific trading hours, research time, and breaks, it indicates that you value discipline and consistency in your trading. Such a routine often leads to better decision-making and performance.

Erratic or Chaotic Schedule: If your response describes a haphazard or unpredictable daily routine, it may suggest a lack of discipline. Trading without a clear schedule can lead to impulsive decisions and erratic results. In this case, implementing a more organized routine may improve your trading outcomes.

Excessive Screen Time: If you find that you spend an excessive amount of time in front of your trading screens, constantly monitoring markets, it could indicate an obsession with trading. While being informed is essential, spending too much time without breaks can lead to burnout and negatively affect your well-being.

No Defined Trading Hours: Some traders may not have specific trading hours and engage in trading activities sporadically throughout the day. This approach can result in missed opportunities and emotional fatigue due to the constant need to make decisions.

Balanced Work-Life Schedule: A trader who balances trading with personal time, exercise, and relaxation demonstrates a healthy approach to trading. This routine indicates a focus on overall well-being and can contribute to better decision-making in the long run.

Prioritizing Learning: If your daily routine includes time for learning, such as reading financial news, studying charts, or practicing trading strategies, it reflects a commitment to continuous improvement. Learning can enhance your trading skills and knowledge over time.

Inadequate Sleep: A lack of adequate sleep due to late-night trading or early market openings can be detrimental to your decision-making abilities. It's crucial to ensure that your daily routine allows for sufficient rest.

Neglecting Personal Relationships: If your trading routine leads to neglecting personal relationships or important commitments, it may indicate an unhealthy obsession with trading. Maintaining a balance between trading and personal life is essential for long-term happiness and well-being.

What's your ideal routine look like?

The Ideal daily routine for a trader is a highly individualized concept, influenced by personal preferences, trading style, and life circumstances. When traders contemplate their ideal routine, they are essentially envisioning a schedule that optimizes their trading performance while maintaining a healthy work-life balance. Here are several possible answers to the question along with their interpretations:

Full-Time Trading Focus:

This trader envisions a daily routine built around dedicating their full attention to trading. For them, trading isn't just a part of life; it is life. They're prepared to immerse themselves in market analysis, research, and trading activities for most of their day. This intense focus reflects a commitment to making trading their primary source of income.

Part-Time Trading Supplement:

In contrast, this trader aims for a more balanced approach, where trading complements their primary job or other income sources. While they appreciate the potential benefits of trading, they don't want to rely solely on it for financial security. This approach offers a way to enjoy the rewards of trading without the pressure of full-time commitment.

Work and Family First:

For some traders, maintaining a 9 to 5 job and prioritizing family commitments is the foundation of their daily routine. Trading takes a backseat when work and family require attention. These traders are comfortable with extended periods of not actively trading or holding positions, often aligning with a positional trading style that requires less frequent monitoring and adjustment. Their routine reflects a balance between their professional career, family responsibilities, and trading aspirations.

Early Morning Trader:

Thriving as an early morning trader, this individual kicks off their day with pre-market analysis and active trading during the market's opening hours. They harness the volatility and news releases characteristic of mornings, aligning their routine with the market's most active period.

Evening Trader:

This trader prioritizes flexibility by trading in the evening, allowing daytime engagement in various interests and commitments. They structure their routine to accommodate a balanced lifestyle while reserving evenings for trading when the market is accessible.

Structured Research Time:

Research and analysis take center stage in this trader's daily routine. They recognize the significance of thorough preparation in trading success and allocate a substantial portion of their schedule to these essential activities.

Scheduled Breaks and Exercise:

Physical and mental well-being are top priorities for this trader. They incorporate regular breaks for exercise and relaxation into their routine to keep their mind and body sharp, acknowledging the importance of stress reduction and maintaining focus.

Adherence to Trading Plan:

For this disciplined trader, sticking to their trading plan is non-negotiable. They follow predefined entry and exit points, risk management rules, and position sizing meticulously. Their routine revolves around ensuring adherence to these critical elements.

Time for Personal Development:

This trader carves out time for personal development and continuous learning. They understand that staying updated and improving trading skills is an ongoing process. Their routine incorporates opportunities for growth and skill enhancement.

Weekend Review and Planning:

Weekends hold a special purpose for this trader. They use this time to review past trades, assess their performance, and plan meticulously for the upcoming trading week. This structured approach allows for continuous improvement and adaptation.

Goal-Oriented Trading:

Goal setting drives this trader's daily routine. Whether it's monthly income targets or long-term financial objectives, their routine serves as a structured pathway to achieve these trading ambitions.

Balanced Lifestyle:

Maintaining a harmonious work-life balance is paramount to this trader. Their ideal routine ensures ample time for personal interests, family, and relaxation, alongside their trading aspirations. Balancing both worlds is a core aspect of their daily life.

There are only a few questions listed here, but we strongly recommend that you take some time to create additional questions, provide detailed answers to them, and thoroughly review and analyze your responses. This process will help you gain deeper insights into your trading mindset and objectives.

Developing Emotional Resilience

Understanding that we're human is a key, having assessed ourselves and established an ideal routine, it's crucial to address how we handle our emotions during unforeseen circumstances in the trading world. When faced with unexpected emotional responses during a open trade, it's essential to have a plan in place. One effective strategy is to recognize the signs of heightened emotions, such as increased heart rate, tension, or anxiety. If you notice these indicators, consider taking immediate action.

Close the Trade and Step Away:

A valuable approach is to promptly close the trade irrespective of trading loss/gain and distance yourself from your trading desk. By doing so, you remove the immediate trigger of your emotional response and give yourself space to regain composure. This action can prevent impulsive decisions influenced by heightened emotions, which often lead to poor trading outcomes.

Taking a Break for Clarity:

Stepping away from your trading station doesn't imply quitting trading altogether. Instead, it's a way to temporarily disengage to regain mental clarity and emotional balance. Use this time to focus on calming activities, such as deep breathing exercises, stretching, or a short walk. This break can help you return to trading with a calmer and more rational mindset.

Reflect and Analyze:

Once you've addressed the emotional trigger and regained composure, take some time to reflect on what caused the emotional reaction. Was it unexpected news, a sudden price swing, or a deviation from your trading plan? Understanding the source of your emotions allows you to make informed adjustments to your strategy or risk management techniques.

Learning from the Experience:

Managing emotions during unexpected periods is a continuous learning process. Each emotional response provides an opportunity to enhance your emotional resilience. By acknowledging and addressing these triggers, you'll gradually become better equipped to handle unexpected situations in the future.

If you do not have any open positions in the first place, just stay on the side lines until the emotions are back on track, remember *"Everyday is an opportunity"* you do not miss anything until you bust your trading account, do not be urged to take a trade until your emotions are subsided.

Maintaining a Trading Journal

In the journey of becoming a successful trader, one invaluable tool that often gets overlooked is the trading journal. Keeping a comprehensive trading journal is not merely an optional task but an essential component of a trader's toolkit.

Understanding the Value:

A trading journal serves as your personal trading diary, documenting every aspect of your trading experiences. It acts as both a historical record and a forward-looking guide. The primary values of maintaining a trading journal are:

Accountability: A journal keeps you accountable for your trading decisions and actions. When you write down your trades and emotions, you're less likely to engage in impulsive or irrational behavior.

Learning Tool: It's a repository of your trading experiences, allowing you to review and learn from past successes and mistakes. Through careful analysis, you can identify patterns in your trading behavior and adapt accordingly.

Emotion Management: A journal helps you track and manage your emotions during trading. By recording your feelings and reactions, you become more self-aware and better equipped to control emotional responses.

Recording Essential Information:

To create an effective trading journal, it's crucial to know what information to record. Here are the key components to include:

Trade Details: Document the specifics of each trade, including entry and exit prices, position size, and the type of trade (buy/sell, options strategy).

Market Conditions: Describe the market environment during the trade, noting factors like volatility, news events, and overall sentiment.

Emotions: Record your emotional state before, during, and after the trade. This helps identify emotional triggers and their impact on your decisions.

Trading Plan Adherence: Assess how well you adhered to your trading plan, including risk management and exit strategies.

Outcome and Analysis: Document the trade's outcome, profit or loss, and any post-trade analysis. Include insights into what went well and what could have been improved.

Noteworthy Events: Make note of any significant market events or news that may have influenced the trade.

Utilizing Journal Entries for Improvement:

Maintaining a trading journal is not just about recording information; it's about leveraging that data for continuous growth. Here's how you can use your journal entries for improvement:

Identify Patterns: Regularly review your journal to identify recurring patterns, whether they relate to successful strategies, emotional triggers, or specific market conditions.

Adjust Strategies: If you notice patterns of success or failure, use this insight to adapt and refine your trading strategies. Likewise, recognize when emotional factors impact your trading decisions and work on mitigating them.

Maintain Discipline: A trading journal reinforces discipline by holding you accountable for following your trading plan. It highlights instances where you deviated from your strategy.

Set Goals: Based on your journal entries, set specific trading goals for improvement. Whether it's reducing emotional reactions or increasing adherence to your plan, having clear objectives facilitates progress.

Track Progress: Over time, review your journal entries to gauge your progress in meeting your trading goals. Celebrate your successes and adjust your strategies for areas that need improvement.

Having a mentor who can review your trading journal and provide constructive feedback is a bonus, it could be your brother who also trades, or a friend or anyone.

A trading journal is a powerful tool for traders of all levels. It helps you maintain discipline, manage emotions, and continuously refine your trading approach. By honestly recording and analyzing your experiences, you can unlock valuable insights that contribute to your growth as a trader and enhance your long-term success.

16: Full-Time Trading: Exploring Every Trader's Dream

The dream of becoming a full-time trader is a common aspiration among traders. This chapter explores the various facets of full-time trading and the psychological, financial, and practical considerations that accompany this endeavor.

The Allure of Full-Time Trading

Many individuals who engage in trading, whether in stocks, options, or other financial instruments, share a common aspiration—to become a full-time trader. This section explores the captivating reasons behind the allure of full-time trading and the factors that drive traders to transition from traditional careers to a life devoted to the financial markets.

Financial Independence: One of the primary reasons traders are drawn to full-time trading is the prospect of achieving financial independence. The ability to generate income directly from trading activities can be liberating, freeing traders from the constraints of a traditional nine-to-five job. They envision a life where their financial destiny is firmly within their own hands, no longer subject to the whims of employers or economic downturns.

Flexibility and Autonomy: Another compelling aspect of full-time trading is the freedom and autonomy it offers. Traders relish the idea of setting their own schedules, choosing when and where to trade, and having the flexibility to adapt to changing market conditions. This flexibility is particularly appealing to those who value work-life balance and desire more control over their daily routines.

The Thrill of Trading: Trading itself can be exhilarating. The adrenaline rush of making split-second decisions, the anticipation of market movements, and the satisfaction of profitable trades create an addictive and thrilling experience. For many traders, the idea of turning this passion into a full-time pursuit is irresistible.

Unlimited Earning Potential: Full-time traders are enticed by the notion of unlimited earning potential. Unlike salaried jobs with fixed incomes, trading offers the possibility of substantial profits. Traders envision the opportunity to exponentially grow their wealth, with the sky as the limit.

Escape from Mundanity: Traditional jobs can sometimes feel monotonous and unfulfilling. Traders see full-time trading as an escape from the mundane routines of corporate life. They crave the intellectual challenge and excitement that trading provides on a daily basis.

The Desire for Entrepreneurship: Full-time trading is often viewed as a form of entrepreneurship. Traders are essentially running their own small businesses, making strategic decisions, managing risk, and aiming for profitability. This entrepreneurial spirit appeals to individuals seeking a more self-directed career path.

Potential for Early Retirement: Some traders aspire to achieve early retirement through full-time trading. They envision building substantial wealth in a shorter timeframe, enabling them to retire earlier than they would in a conventional career. This early retirement goal serves as a powerful motivator.

Passion for Financial Markets: Finally, a deep passion for the financial markets drives many individuals toward full-time trading. These individuals genuinely enjoy studying market trends, analyzing data, and seeking out profitable opportunities. For them, trading is not just a means to an end but a fulfilling and enriching pursuit in itself.

The Decision-Making Process

Transitioning from part-time or occasional trading to full-time trading is a significant decision that should not be taken lightly. To make an informed choice, traders must thoroughly evaluate various critical factors that will impact their success and well-being in the world of full-time trading. This section explores the key considerations that should guide a trader's decision-making process.

Financial Stability: The cornerstone of transitioning to full-time trading is financial stability. Traders need to assess whether they have a sufficient financial cushion to support themselves and their families during potential periods of trading losses or market volatility. This includes having an emergency fund, paying off high-interest debts, and ensuring ongoing access to healthcare and other essential services. Adequate financial preparation is vital to weather the inevitable ups and downs of trading.

Risk Tolerance: Full-time trading carries inherent risks, and traders must honestly evaluate their risk tolerance. Assessing one's ability to cope with the emotional and financial stress of trading is crucial. Traders should ask themselves how they would react to significant losses, drawdowns, or unexpected market events. A realistic understanding of their risk tolerance can prevent impulsive decisions and emotional trading.

Trading Skills and Knowledge: Before making the leap to full-time trading, traders should assess their trading skills and knowledge. This involves evaluating their proficiency in technical analysis, fundamental analysis, risk management, and trade execution. Full-time trading demands a higher level of competence and confidence in one's trading abilities, as there is no safety net of a regular paycheck.

Long-Term Goals: Traders should consider their long-term goals and whether full-time trading aligns with those objectives. It's essential to clarify what they aim to achieve through trading—whether it's financial independence, early retirement, or a particular lifestyle. Full-time trading should be seen as a means to an end, rather than an end in itself, and should fit into a broader life plan.

Trading Strategy and Track Record: A well-defined trading strategy with a proven track record is a prerequisite for full-time trading. Traders must assess whether their trading approach is consistently profitable and sustainable over time. Backtesting, risk-adjusted returns, and performance metrics should guide this evaluation. A robust strategy provides a higher degree of confidence in the viability of full-time trading.

Psychological Preparedness: Full-time trading can be mentally taxing. Traders should evaluate their psychological readiness to cope with the emotional challenges of trading. This includes managing stress, fear, and greed, as well as maintaining discipline and mental resilience during losing streaks. Developing a trading mindset that can withstand the psychological pressures of full-time trading is crucial.

Market Conditions and Volatility: The overall market conditions and volatility levels should also influence the decision to trade full-time. Traders should be aware of the current economic environment, geopolitical factors, and market trends. Entering full-time trading during periods of extreme uncertainty or volatility may pose higher risks.

Backup Plans and Contingencies: It's prudent to have backup plans and contingencies in place. Full-time traders should consider what they would do in case of extended trading losses or unforeseen circumstances that prevent them from trading. Having alternative income sources, part-time work, or freelance opportunities can provide a safety net.

Legal and Regulatory Compliance: Full-time traders should ensure they are compliant with all legal and regulatory requirements, including tax obligations. Understanding tax implications and seeking professional advice is essential to avoid any legal complications.

Lifestyle Adjustments: Finally, traders must be prepared for lifestyle adjustments. Full-time trading often involves irregular working hours, isolation, and a shift in daily routines. Traders should discuss these changes with their families and ensure they are comfortable with the lifestyle implications.

Family and Social Considerations

The decision to transition to full-time trading isn't just a personal one; it often has a significant impact on a trader's family and social life. Acknowledging and addressing family and social considerations is crucial to ensuring a harmonious transition into full-time trading.

The Role of Family and Social Support: Full-time trading can be emotionally demanding, and having a support system in place is invaluable. Traders should communicate their aspirations and plans with their family members and close friends. Supportive loved ones can provide encouragement, understanding, and a safety net during challenging times. Open and honest conversations about the commitment required for full-time trading help set expectations and foster a supportive environment.

Challenges in Communication: It's common for traders to encounter challenges in communicating the intricacies of trading to their families and friends who may not be familiar with the financial markets. Explaining the volatile nature of trading, the possibility of losses, and the time commitment involved is essential. Traders should be patient and empathetic when addressing concerns and questions from their loved ones. Encouraging them to learn about trading or involving them in discussions about financial goals can foster mutual understanding.

Balancing Personal Time: Full-time trading often requires dedicated screen time and research. Traders should be mindful of balancing their trading commitments with their personal lives. Prioritizing quality time with family and friends is essential to maintaining healthy relationships. Effective time management, setting boundaries, and scheduling regular breaks can help strike a balance between trading and personal life.

Financial Communication: Financial transparency is crucial when transitioning into full-time trading. Spouses or significant others should be involved in financial discussions and decisions. Traders should provide clarity on the potential impact of trading on household finances, including the allocation of trading capital and risk management strategies. Collaborative financial planning ensures that everyone is on the same page and can help alleviate financial stress.

Emergency Plans: It's prudent to have contingency plans in place to address unexpected financial challenges. Traders should discuss contingency measures, such as what to do in the event of a significant drawdown or loss of trading income. Establishing emergency funds or alternative income sources can provide peace of mind and financial security for the family.

Support Groups and Communities: Traders can explore local or online trading communities and support groups. These communities offer a platform for sharing experiences, seeking advice, and connecting with others who understand the challenges and rewards of full-time trading. Engaging with like-minded individuals can be empowering and provide a sense of belonging.

Monitoring Stress and Well-being: Full-time trading can be stressful, and traders should be vigilant about their mental and emotional well-being. It's essential to have strategies in place to manage stress effectively. This may include regular exercise, mindfulness practices, and seeking professional counseling or therapy if needed. Healthy traders are better equipped to navigate the emotional demands of trading and maintain positive relationships.

Maintaining a Work-Life Balance: Full-time traders should consciously strive for a work-life balance that aligns with their values and priorities. Allocating time for personal interests, hobbies, and social activities is vital for overall well-being. Prioritizing self-care and relaxation contributes to emotional resilience and enhances the trader's ability to make sound decisions.

Maintaining Discipline

Maintaining discipline is one of the most significant challenges that full-time traders face, primarily because they often lack the traditional work structure and accountability found in regular employment. Staying disciplined in a trading career demands a unique set of strategies and habits to ensure consistent success.

Understanding the Discipline Dilemma: The absence of a conventional office environment, a boss, or fixed working hours can create a discipline dilemma for full-time traders. Without external supervision, traders must rely on self-discipline to maintain focus and execute trading plans consistently.

Creating a Trading Routine: Establishing a daily trading routine is essential for maintaining discipline. Traders should set specific work hours and adhere to them consistently. This routine helps create a sense of structure and separates trading from personal life, reducing the risk of distractions.

Developing a Trading Plan: A comprehensive trading plan acts as a roadmap for full-time traders. It outlines trading strategies, risk management rules, entry and exit criteria, and other essential guidelines. Traders must commit to following their trading plans rigorously, avoiding impulsive decisions.

Accountability Measures: To counter the lack of external accountability, traders can implement self-accountability measures. This may include sharing trading goals and progress with a mentor, coach, or trading community. Accountability partners can help ensure traders adhere to their plans and remain disciplined.

Managing Distractions: Distractions can be detrimental to discipline. Traders should create a dedicated trading environment that minimizes interruptions and external diversions. Turning off social media, news alerts, and non-essential notifications during trading hours can enhance focus.

Avoiding Overtrading: Overtrading, driven by the temptation to maximize profits, is a common undisciplined behavior. Full-time traders should establish daily trading limits and adhere to them rigorously. Once these limits are reached, traders should step away from the screens to prevent impulsive decisions.

Continuous Education: Staying informed and educated about financial markets is a vital component of trading discipline. Traders should allocate time for ongoing learning, research, and staying updated with market developments. Continuous education enhances decision-making and boosts confidence.

Maintaining Emotional Balance: Emotional regulation is intertwined with discipline. Traders must be aware of their emotions and employ techniques like mindfulness and stress management to maintain emotional balance. Emotional turbulence can lead to impulsive decisions and undisciplined trading behavior.

Review and Adaptation: Regularly reviewing trading performance is essential for maintaining discipline. Traders should assess their trades, analyze what worked and what didn't, and adjust their strategies accordingly. A commitment to self-improvement and adaptability helps reinforce discipline.

Taking Breaks: Just as in any profession, full-time traders require breaks to recharge and maintain discipline. Short breaks during trading hours and longer vacations at regular intervals prevent burnout and allow traders to return to their work with renewed focus.

Seeking Mentorship: Having a mentor or coach can significantly contribute to discipline. A mentor provides guidance, accountability, and a wealth of experience. Their insights and feedback can help traders stay disciplined and make informed decisions.

Journaling and Record-Keeping: Maintaining a trading journal to record thoughts, emotions, and trade outcomes fosters discipline. The journal serves as a reflective tool, enabling traders to identify patterns of behavior and maintain accountability.

Full Time Trading: Trader Case Studies
Trader Story 1: The Reality Check - From Overconfidence to a Humbling Comeback

Jamie was a dreamer. Armed with just enough knowledge to be dangerous and suffering from the Dunning-Kruger effect, he was convinced that quitting his job to become a full-time trader was the path to quick riches. His monthly salary of 40,000 INR seemed like small change compared to the vast opportunities he believed trading would offer.

With 5 lakhs in savings, Jamie dove headfirst into the world of trading. He had grand visions of consistently earning 40,000 INR every month, imagining that his savings would sustain him indefinitely. However, he was oblivious to the harsh reality of the markets.

During his first month as a trader, Jamie managed to eke out a profit of 10,000 INR. While it was a modest gain, it fueled his unwarranted confidence. Jamie began to dream bigger, setting his sights on a staggering 70,000 INR for the following month. He ignored the fact that his initial profit was a mere fraction of what he had hoped to achieve.

Driven by unrealistic expectations, Jamie started taking reckless risks. He leveraged his trades to the max and ventured into highly volatile markets. Unfortunately, luck was not on his side, and his trading account began to hemorrhage money.

By the end of the second month, Jamie's once-promising trading account had been wiped clean. He had lost every last rupee of his hard-earned savings. The dream of becoming a full-time trader had turned into a devastating financial nightmare.

But Jamie was not one to stay down for long. He realized that trading was far more complex and challenging than he had initially thought. He decided to put his ego aside and return to a stable job, grateful that such an opportunity awaited him.

Jamie spent the next few years rebuilding his financial foundation, starting from scratch. He learned valuable lessons about the importance of patience, discipline, and realistic expectations. He also continued to educate himself about trading, this time with a more cautious approach.

Over time, Jamie's savings grew once more, albeit steadily and cautiously. He no longer harbored illusions of quick riches, but he had gained something even more valuable—wisdom and humility.

Jamie's story serves as a cautionary tale for those who underestimate the complexities of trading and the importance of acquiring the necessary skills and knowledge before taking the leap. His journey from overconfidence to a humbling comeback is a testament to the resilience of the human spirit and the enduring power of lessons learned the hard way.

Trader Story 2: A Journey of Self Discovery

Siba had dedicated more than 15 years of his life to a successful career in the IT industry. His reputation preceded him—known for his unwavering commitment, punctuality, and impressive knowledge. Yet, beneath the facade of a dedicated IT professional,

Siba harbored another dream—one that involved trading in the world of options.

For 15 years, Siba had masterfully balanced his corporate job with part-time options trading. His prudent financial management had allowed him to accumulate a substantial emergency fund, clear all debts, and even become a homeowner. With his financial security in place, Siba saw an opportunity to fulfill his dream of full-time trading and reclaim the precious commodity of time.

After thorough discussions with his family and rigorous self-evaluation, Siba took the leap into full-time options trading. He said his goodbyes to the IT company that had been his professional home for over a decade and stepped into the uncharted territory of self-employment.

However, the transition was not as smooth as he had anticipated. The absence of a manager and the structure of a corporate environment led to an unexpected challenge—Siba struggled to maintain discipline. He found himself disregarding the punctuality that had been his hallmark for 15 years, often oversleeping and losing precious trading hours.

Despite dedicating more time to trading than ever before, Siba's profits dwindled. It was a frustrating revelation, and he couldn't ignore the fact that he had been overtrading in a desperate attempt to match his previous income. Stress and anxiety took hold of him, casting a shadow over his once-promising trading journey.

After a period of introspection and careful consideration, Siba made a pivotal decision. He withdrew his trading capital and invested it wisely in a fixed deposit, ensuring his financial stability. Realizing that structure and discipline were integral to his success, he actively began searching for a new job.

To his surprise, Siba faced a challenging job market. Opportunities that matched his previous income were scarce. Faced with a stark reality, he chose to prioritize financial stability over the allure of full-time trading. Siba accepted a modest-paying job, a far cry from his previous salary.

Although the transition was humbling, Siba approached his new job with the same dedication and professionalism that had defined his corporate career. While the world of full-time trading had eluded him, he found contentment and a renewed sense of purpose in his new professional journey.

Siba's story is a testament to the importance of adaptability and resilience when navigating unexpected life changes. While his full-time trading aspiration may not have panned out as expected, he embraced a new path that ultimately led to financial stability and a newfound appreciation for the value of time.

Trader Story 3: Decade Long Journey - The Road to Full-Time Trading

Sundar's journey in the world of trading was a remarkable testament to the transformative power of dedication and discipline. He had embarked on this journey at the tender age of 18, starting with pocket money and a curiosity that soon evolved into a life-changing skill. As he approached his 10th year in the IT industry, he also celebrated 18 years of trading experience, cultivating a unique blend of expertise that combined buying and selling options.

Sundar wasn't just a trader; he was a trader with a meticulous routine that reflected his deep commitment to the craft. Each day began with rigorous exercise to maintain both physical and mental fitness. He religiously planned and journaled every trade, documenting not just the financial aspects but also his emotional state at various stages of each trade.

Despite his wealth of experience and evident skill, Sundar found himself in a perplexing situation in his IT job. The salary he received did not match the level of expertise he had developed over the years. He yearned to transition into full-time trading, a move he believed would not only free up his time but also align his professional life with his true passion.

However, there was one significant hurdle in his path—his family, particularly his wife, was not convinced about the viability of full-time trading. They were wary of the financial uncertainty it might bring. Sundar, deeply committed to his family's well-being, knew he needed to strike a balance between his dreams and his responsibilities.

After numerous heartfelt discussions with his family, a compromise was reached. Sundar agreed to continue working in the IT sector for two more years while consistently earning enough to cover the family's expenses. This was a test of his abilities, a challenge he willingly accepted.

For two years, Sundar meticulously executed his cunning discipline in both his IT job and trading endeavors. He stayed true to his commitment, ensuring that his trading profits consistently covered the family's expenditures. This demonstrated his unwavering dedication to the promise he had made.

As the two-year milestone approached, Sundar's consistency paid off. He had not only met but exceeded the financial targets he had set for himself and his family. The moment of truth arrived, and Sundar was finally ready to make the leap into full-time trading.

The transition was met with mixed emotions. While there was undoubtedly excitement about pursuing his true passion, there was also the uncertainty that accompanied such a significant change. Yet, with 18 years of trading experience and a proven track record of financial responsibility, Sundar was well-prepared for this new chapter in his life.

Becoming a full-time trader came with its fair share of ups and downs. The initial months were challenging as he adjusted to the new lifestyle and financial responsibilities. There were moments of doubt and anxiety, but Sundar's discipline and resilience shone through. He meticulously managed his finances, adhered to his trading strategies, and continued his commitment to self-improvement.

Gradually, the tide began to turn. Sundar's consistent efforts bore fruit, and he started to see a steady stream of profits from his trading activities. He refined his strategies, learned from both successes and setbacks, and honed his skills as a full-time trader.

Over the years, Sundar not only maintained financial stability but also achieved a level of trading success that surpassed his expectations. His family, initially apprehensive, celebrated his accomplishments and unwavering dedication.

Sundar's journey from a young trader with pocket money to a seasoned professional balancing two careers was a testament to his unwavering commitment, discipline, and the support of his family. As he stepped into the world of full-time trading, he did so with gratitude for the lessons he had learned along the way and a determination to succeed in his true calling.

It's worth noting that full time trading is not for everyone, if it was easy you wouldn't find anyone working 9 to 5 but still the majority works at normal labour force, majority of traders lose money in the markets. You may say you know a personal friend who makes a living out of trading and being very successful, what you miss to consider is thousands of failed traders per successful trader, this is also known as survivorship bias, decide wisely.

17. Traders' Testimony

This chapter is dedicated to sharing real-life testimonials and stories from traders who have navigated the complexities of the financial markets. These traders come from diverse backgrounds, experiences, and trading styles, providing insights into their journeys, successes, challenges, and the lessons they've learned along the way.

A Trader's Journey from Losses to Wisdom

I'm Rajesh, and my journey in the trading world has been filled with ups and downs. I ventured into the markets during my teenage years, initially starting with equities trading before gradually stepping into the realm of options trading. Unfortunately, my early experiences were marred by significant losses, almost wiping out three years' worth of income. Frustrated and disheartened, I made the tough decision to walk away from trading for the next five years.

During this hiatus, I took the time to save up some capital and reflect on my past mistakes. When I eventually returned to the markets, I was determined not to repeat my previous blunders. It soon became evident that my initial failures were a result of trading without a clear plan or system. I had been making decisions impulsively, driven by news snippets and relying on random technical indicators. Most importantly, I had ignored the impact of my emotions on my trading decisions.

Recognizing the need for a comprehensive education, I embarked on a journey of self-improvement in the world of trading. I started from the ground up, immersing myself in the fundamentals of call and put options, and grasping the basics of various trading strategies. It became painfully clear that I had been trading blindly, without a solid foundation of knowledge and strategy.

As time went by, I slowly gained the wisdom and expertise needed for successful options trading. I began to see profitable returns on my investments, and my trading account started to grow. However, I couldn't help but carry the weight of regret for my earlier losses. Those losses had the potential to transform my life positively, and I couldn't help but wonder how different my financial journey could have been if I had started with the right knowledge and mindset from the beginning.

Family, Finance, and the Journey to Success

I'm Ganesh, and my journey in the world of finance and trading has been nothing short of a roller coaster ride. Growing up in a challenging environment with a single mother working tirelessly to support our family while my father battled alcoholism, I understood the importance of financial stability from a very young age.

After completing my bachelor's degree, I took up a 9-to-5 job with a meager salary. While it was a relief to contribute to my family's income, I knew I had greater responsibilities, including educating my two younger siblings. The traditional path to financial stability felt arduous, and I began searching desperately for alternative sources of income online.

That's when I stumbled upon options trading, a world I knew little about. Fueled by the desire to provide a better life for my family, I hastily delved into options trading without fully grasping the basics. It was a risky move, but I felt compelled to explore this potential opportunity.

One fateful month, my credit card bill arrived, and it was shockingly high. I was certain that I hadn't spent irresponsibly; the bulk of the expenses went towards my family's education and other necessities. However, the total bill exceeded my entire monthly salary. With just ten days to make the payment, I made a bold decision – I would try to trade my way out of this financial predicament.

Unfortunately, my initial foray into trading was fraught with losses. My lack of knowledge and experience led to a series of poor decisions, and I ended up losing everything I had invested. It was a devastating blow, and I felt the weight of my financial obligations pressing down on me.

To pay off my credit card debt and continue providing for my family, I had no choice but to take out another loan. I remember locking myself in my room, tears streaming down my face, and silently grappling with the immense pressure and disappointment I felt.

Years have passed since those dark times, and my life has undergone a remarkable transformation. I persevered, learned from my mistakes, and committed myself to both my regular job and the world of options trading. Today, I find myself in a stable and secure financial position, and all my siblings have received the education they deserved.

While these memories of financial struggle still resurface when I hear others facing similar challenges, they serve as a reminder of the resilience and determination that brought me to where I am today. My journey through options trading has not only secured my family's future but has also given me the strength to overcome adversity and achieve success.

From Software Engineer to Algo Trading Success

I'm Bala, and I have a background in software engineering. While working in the finance industry, I couldn't help but notice how some of my colleagues were consistently making money through options trading. Their discussions piqued my curiosity, and I decided to delve into the world of finance. With little prior knowledge, I began learning the basics of options trading and various strategies.

As my understanding of trading grew, I became increasingly excited about the potential financial gains. I invested a substantial amount of money in trading, hoping to see significant returns. However, as I started trading actively, I experienced a rollercoaster of emotions with every price movement in the market. It was clear that my emotional responses were impacting my trading decisions.

Recognizing the need for a more systematic approach, I embarked on a journey of research and self-education. I began developing a trading algorithm that would autonomously execute predefined strategies based on specific criteria. This algorithmic approach brought about a remarkable transformation in my trading experience.

The algorithm proved to be a game-changer, consistently generating income month after month. While occasional losses were inevitable, when I looked at the bigger picture over a year's time, the algorithm consistently delivered more than a 20% return on my investments. What was even more satisfying was that this automated trading approach required minimal monitoring, allowing me to free up valuable time.

Over the course of 12 years of algo trading, my wealth has significantly increased. I can't help but reflect on the importance of conducting thorough research and learning from others before diving into the trading world. I'm immensely grateful to my colleagues whose discussions initially sparked my interest in options trading, ultimately leading me to a better financial situation and greater financial freedom.

Cautionary Tale of Overleveraging and Greed in Options Trading

I'm Mark, and I began my journey into options trading while working at an entry-level position in a finance company. Full of ambition and eager to make a significant profit, I decided to borrow a substantial amount of one million rupees to invest in the options market. My initial goal was modest: I aimed to make just one rupee more than the interest amount, believing that even this small gain would be profitable and provide me with valuable trading experience.

I set my monthly target at 10,000 rupees, which represented a conservative 1% return on my total capital. Consistently, I managed to exceed this goal, earning around 11,000 rupees every month. I was content with this steady progress, considering the additional 1,000 rupees as a bonus on top of what I had initially anticipated. However, this initial success sparked a sense of greed within me.

Driven by the desire to increase my profits quickly, I began taking higher risks in my trades. It was a moment of recklessness that led to a significant loss of 50,000 rupees in one unfortunate month. This loss not only wiped out all the profits I had accumulated but also left me in a dire situation. Determined to recover my losses, I set an ambitious target of making 60,000 rupees the following month.

Unfortunately, my desperation to regain what I had lost only led to more substantial losses. My stress levels soared, and I felt trapped in a cycle of escalating debt. Fearful of being judged or criticized, I kept my predicament to myself, which only intensified the emotional burden I was carrying. Despite my best efforts, I continued incurring losses until my trading account was completely wiped out.

The consequences were severe, and I found myself in a serious debt trap. Nearly 90% of my income went towards servicing the EMI for the borrowed capital, and it took years to clear this debt. This painful experience taught me a harsh lesson: borrowing money to trade in the financial markets can be a form of financial suicide. It's a mistake I will never repeat, and it has fundamentally shaped my approach to trading and financial responsibility.

CONCLUSION

As we wrap up our exploration of Options Trading Psychology, it's time to reflect on the intricate interplay of human emotions and trading decisions that we've uncovered throughout this journey. This book has offered a wealth of insights, strategies, and real-life experiences to guide traders through the emotional landscape of options trading.

We began by delving deep into the trader's psyche, gaining a better understanding of how our minds operate when navigating the complex world of financial markets. The lessons we've learned from each chapter are invaluable in helping us strike the right balance in our trading endeavors.

We've examined the powerful influence of emotions like greed and fear, recognizing their potential to either propel us to success or lead us down a path of financial peril. Our journey has highlighted the critical importance of maintaining equilibrium in our approach to risk-taking.

Throughout this book, we've explored the fascinating realm of cognitive biases and fallacies, shedding light on the ways in which our thought processes can lead us astray. Armed with this knowledge, we are better equipped to avoid the common psychological traps that traders often fall into.

The delicate equilibrium between hope and realism has been a recurring theme, emphasizing the need to temper our optimism with a firm grounding in reality. Regret has shown us the power of learning from our mistakes, transforming setbacks into opportunities for growth.

We've placed a strong emphasis on trading discipline and patience, as well as strategies for navigating losses and recovering from drawdowns. Our journey even took us into the inner workings of the trader's brain, unraveling the intricate neurochemical processes that influence our trading decisions.

Whether your aspirations involve becoming a full-time trader, executing trades with unwavering conviction, or striking a harmonious balance between trading and personal life, the insights provided in this book have equipped you with the tools to make well-informed decisions aligned with your unique goals and values.

The personal testimonies shared throughout this journey serve as a poignant reminder that every trader's path is uniquely challenging and triumphant in its own way. While we cannot adopt every piece of advice or strategy, we have the power to choose what resonates most with us and customize our trading psychology accordingly.

Ultimately, as we conclude, remember that we are all human, and emotions are an integral part of the trading experience. Successful traders distinguish themselves by their ability to understand and manage these emotions effectively. As you embark on your options trading journey, keep in mind that it's not just about mastering the markets but also mastering yourself. Stay curious, stay disciplined, and stay true to your trading psychology plan. May your path to trading success be both enlightening and financially rewarding.

Thank you for purchasing this book and reading it to the end!

Please follow **"Karthik MUTHUMOHAN"** on amazon for future updates on promotions, new releases, and updates in the book.

If this material helped you, **please leave a positive review on amazon.**

If this material was not helpful, please write to us at karthick.gill@gmail.com so we can improve based on your feedback.

www.ingramcontent.com/pod-product-compliance
Lightning Source LLC
Chambersburg PA
CBHW072155290526
45794CB00004B/1519